HYMNS AND THEIR USES

A Guide to Improved Congregational Singing

James Rawlings Sydnor

AGAPE
Carol Stream, Illinois 60187

FOREWORD

For thirty-five years I have had the pleasure of Jim Sydnor's friendship, counsel, and guidance in the area of hymnody, and I am honored to contribute a foreword to his latest contribution to the betterment of congregational hymn singing.

Through his work as a churchman, teacher, musician, administrator, author, editor of hymnals, and writer of articles for many publications, Dr. Sydnor has developed a practical working philosophy of how to go about the task of making hymn singing more effective and meaningful. In an earlier book, *The Hymn and Congregational Singing,* he outlined a helpful program for a church. In his series of four articles for *The Hymn* he further developed these ideas. Now, in this latest book, he offers a quintessential program of inestimable value to ministers, church musicians, worship leaders, and plain "pew people."

We can all be grateful for his continued thought and writing and for the insights of a lifetime of reading, studying, thinking, playing, singing, and planning.

Austin C. Lovelace
Denver, Colorado
August, 1981

PREFACE

This book is written to assist church musicians, ministers, and committees of worship to achieve better congregational singing, and to guide students in classes in hymnology and general church music.

There is in almost every person a deep spring of song waiting to be released. A few years ago Alan Villiers was in Cardiff, the capital of Wales. Above the noise of traffic, he heard the singing of a vast crowd of men. Upon inquiry, he learned that an international rugby game was about to begin in a nearby stadium.

> I made for the arena. It was packed, but I found a place in a window of a building nearby where I could see and hear. The crowd was singing hymns. No cheerleaders—no organization at all. They all just sang perfectly together, as if they had been practicing since birth—60,000 men, mostly in cloth caps, from mine and steel-rolling mill, office, shop, and farm, from university and technological college. I felt I was listening to the spirit of Wales.[1]

The quality and quantity of hymn singing in the United States has not kept up with the quality and quantity of hymns and hymnals. Within the past several decades, each of the major denominations has published a new hymnal. Without exception, the editorial committees have kept a nucleus of "old favorites." They have not only rechecked the hymnic treasures of the past but they have also diligently sought out new texts and tunes, either from recent hymnals of sister denominations or by commissioning their own original hymns.

Also the ministers have probably been trained in seminaries

1. From "Wales, Land of Bards," by Alan Villiers, *National Geographic*, June 1965. Used by permission.

where chapel worship and perhaps a hymnology class has exposed them to a large repertoire of hymns. Staff musicians likewise may have gained an acquaintance with new hymns at music conferences and schools.

When these concerned local church leaders attempt to introduce their new hymnals and to improve congregational singing in general, they need great skill, tact, knowledge, and patience in order to loose the spirit of song in their people. I trust this book can help in this rewarding project. I have tried to keep in mind the needs and traditions of various denominations.

The Hymn Society of America has graciously granted permission for me to use material from my articles which appeared in the 1980 issues of *The Hymn*. When a hymn title or tune name has been cited, I have, as a rule, indicated the location in certain major hymnals where these hymns or tunes can be examined. Here are the hymnals and the abbreviation:

B *Baptist Hymnal* 1975
M Methodist *The Book of Hymns* 1964, 1966
L *Lutheran Book of Worship* 1978
P Presbyterian *The Hymnbook* 1955
E *Ecumenical Praise* 1977 Agape
C *Choirbook for Saints and Singers* 1980 Agape
RC Roman Catholic *Worship II* 1975

James Rawlings Sydnor
Richmond, Virginia
November 1981

CONTENTS

Chapter I

WHO DEVELOPS CONGREGATIONAL SINGING?

Who is responsible for developing congregational singing? Every individual in the congregation!

The person in the pew who sings heartily and thoughtfully every time a hymn is announced is directly promoting this musical offering. The parent who sings a hymn stanza while tucking a child in bed is helping create a lifelong affection for, and dependence on, hymns. The church school teacher who refers to hymn texts to underscore and elucidate lessons is laying a foundation for singing hymns with understanding.

Obviously the more influential post a person has, the greater is his or her responsibility in the area of hymn singing. The minister, the staff musician, the worship committee, the christian education committee—each is charged with some of this responsibility. But it is a fact of life that ministers lead extremely busy professional lives—preaching, counseling, studying, administering and visiting. Organist/choirmasters are sometimes just that—organists and choir directors. The major portion of their time and thought is given to study of choral music and to the recruitment, training, and direction of a number of choirs. Organ practice eats up another sizable amount of time. If anything is to be slighted, congregational music is the most vulnerable. If the people want to sing, good. If they don't, too bad.

Therefore, if the magnificent benefits of great congregational singing are to be appropriated, a firm decision must be made to

Hymn text and tune references are keyed to the following hymnals: B *Baptist Hymnal* 1975, M Methodist *Book of Hymns* 1966, L *Lutheran Book of Worship* 1978, P Presbyterian *The Hymnbook* 1955, E *Ecumenical Praise* 1977 Agape, C *Choirbook for Saints and Singers* 1980 Agape, RC Roman Catholic *Worship II* 1975.

adopt a sensible development plan, assign tasks and periodically assess progress.

How can this be done? Some one in the congregation with a vision of the advantages of excellent congregational singing must be found to set brush fires of enthusiasm. It may be the musician or the minister or some lay person. To do the job efficiently, you will need more than one brain and one person's efforts. Therefore, I suggest the appointment of a committee or task force with the specific and long-term job of developing the congregation's ability to sing hymns and the other service music.

The congregation by its own approved procedures should appoint such a committee charged with developing congregational singing. The minister and musician should belong to this group not only to assist in drawing up realistic productive plans but also to monitor their implementation. It seems desirable to produce a written plan, perhaps for a three-year period, with specific projects and goals to be achieved at specified intervals during this period. Then, perhaps at three- or six-month intervals, the committee should meet to hear reports and assess results and, if necessary, to change plans and reassign responsibilities. It goes without saying that the chairperson should be one who is enthusiastic about the potential of hymns in the lives of the people and who has the knack of firm, tactful, and patient leadership.

Here in telegraphic size is a checklist of projects, each of which could help prime the pump and encourage the congregation to take more interest in the hymns. Check the ones which you think you could use. Most of these items are discussed in considerable detail in later chapters.

1. *Hymn of the month.*☐Some denominations select and publish an annual list of twelve hymns to be studied, learned and sung, one each month. It is usually taught, if unfamiliar, on the first Sunday of the month, by having some description of the hymn's background included either in the bulletin or given from the pulpit. If the tune is unfamiliar, the children and adult choirs could sing it as an anthem before the congregation is asked to participate. The text could be printed in the bulletin and the people requested to use it in their private devotions, to sing it as a family, and perhaps to memorize it. Obviously it would be repeated in public worship several times during the

month. Once learned, these hymns should be repeated during
the following months.

If the denominational list does not exactly suit the local needs,
adapt it. If there is no denominational list, compile your own.
These hymns of the month should maintain a happy balance
between the unfamiliar and the familiar.

2. *A hymn playing class.*□The pianists in various church
school classes would profit by several sessions in which basics of
hymn playing could be explained and demonstrated. Some of
these techniques are described in Chapter 8.

3. *Give the congregation hymn information.*□The persons who
the pews frequently have their interest in hymns whetted by
learning facts about hymn backgrounds, how and why they were
written, origin of tune names, scriptural bases for the text, and
data about authors and composers. Handbooks giving this information are listed in the bibliography. This information can be
printed occasionally or regularly in the service bulletin or can be
given verbally when announcing the hymn. This sharing of information usually should be succinct. During a worship service
the congregation does not need a lengthy lecture on a particular
hymn. However, in leading hymn sings when I have told brief
interesting items about a hymn, I have frequently been thanked
by the singers for sharing these facts.

4. *A hymn festival.*□A hymn festival is a celebration of the
faith through congregational song. Usually lasting about an
hour, it can be planned and sponsored by a local congregation, a
group of churches in a city or region, or a denomination. Hundreds of these events are held across the country each year. A
hymn festival is a strong stimulus for singing in a local church.
Chapter 16 is devoted to explaining how to organize and conduct
these festivals.

5. *Hymn textbooks in the church library.*□Many churches
have an extensive lending library of books on theology, biblical
commentaries, worship, church history, missions and the like.
See to it that a section on hymnody is added, advertised and
read. This section could include such items as hymn histories,
collections of hymn stories, manuals on the use of hymns plus
some representative good hymnals. By all means have your
church library subscribe to *The Hymn,* the official quarterly
journal of The Hymn Society of America, Wittenberg University, Springfield, OH 45501. The bibliography at the end of this

book will give starred suggestions of a basic hymnological library.

6. *Getting a hymnal in every home.*☐Encourage the private ownership of hymnals so that hymns can be read, played and sung at home. Until this is done, congregational singing can never reach its highest level. At the time of the Reformation, many hymnals were pocket sized for convenient transportation between home and church. Both Chapters 11 and 12 discuss the rationale and procedures for accomplishing this project.

7. *Dramatizing hymns.*☐Hymn backgrounds and meanings frequently offer material for dramatization. These plays and pageants can be part of a special hymn singing event or a church night supper. Perhaps a talented member of your congregation could write one.

As an example, be sure to examine *The Singing Bishop* which is a dramatized interpretation of the Palm Sunday hymn "All glory, laud, and honor." (B39,M424,L108,P187,RC9) Composed by Hal H. Hobson, it is a unique and delightful children's drama with a small cast of characters, keyboard and optional other instruments, children's or youth choirs and congregation. It is published by the Choristers Guild, P.O. Box 38188, Dallas, TX 75238 in full score A-200 and chorus part A-200c.

8. *Service the aging and shut-ins with hymns.*☐Church groups are becoming increasingly sensitive to the needs of the aging and shut-ins. Several years ago the Hymn Society of America cooperated with the National Retired Teachers Association and the American Association of Retired Persons in encouraging the writing of hymns celebrating the later years of life and the meaning of aging. Out of 1200 submitted texts, ten have been published by the Hymn Society of America under the title *10 New Hymns on Aging and the Later Years*.

Here is a recent hymn which does not appear in this collection but which addresses a concern that is in the background (or foreground) of everyone's consciousness, especially those in the later years of life. Fred Kaan (1929-) writes directly and wholesomely about death. The music by Jane Marshall sensitively supports the text.

This hymn brings to mind Bishop Thomas Ken's (1637-1711) stanza from his famous Evening hymn, "All Praise to Thee, My

Today I Live

HEARTBEAT: 10.11.10.11.

Fred Kaan, 1929-   Jane Marshall, 1924-

1. To - day I live, but once shall come my death;
2. How I shall die, or when, I do not know,
3. When earth - ly life shall close, as close it must,
4. Mean - while I live and move and I am glad,

1. one day shall still my laugh - ter and my cry - ing,
2. nor where, for end - less is the world's ho - ri - zon;
3. let Je - sus be my broth - er and my mer - it.
4. en - joy this life and all its in - ter - weav - ing:

1. bring to a halt my heart - beat and my breath: Lord,
2. but save me, Lord from thoughts that lay me low, from
3. Let me with - out re - gret re - call the past, then,
4. each giv - en day, as I take up the thread, let

1. give me faith for liv - ing and for dy - ing.
2. mor - bid fears that freeze my power of rea - son.
3. Lord, in - to your hands com - mit my spir - it.
4. love sug - gest my mode, my mood of liv - ing.

God, This Night", (B43, M493, L278, P63, RC16) with its two fundamental prayers: "Teach me to live . . . Teach me to die."

> Teach me to live, that I may dread
> The grave as little as my bed;
> Teach me to die, that so I may
> Rise glorious at the Judgment Day.

The Lutherans, Southern Baptists, United Methodists, and Presbyterians, among others, have hymnals in large print. Here is an actual size sample:

BEAUTIFUL SAVIOR

**1. Beautiful Savior,
King of Creation,
Son of God and Son of Man!
Truly I'd love thee,
Truly I'd serve thee,
Light of my soul, my joy, my crown.**

Some hymnals are printed in Braille. The Library of Congress, Division for the Blind and Physically Handicapped, Washington, DC 20542 makes large-print and Braille hymnals available on loan free of charge to the blind or visually handicapped.

9. *Establish a lending library of hymn recordings.*□Many public and college libraries offer the benefits of lending collections of records and cassettes. Since many families of your congregation have phonographs and cassette players, select some hymn recordings of high quality and make them available through the church's library to your congregation. Here are some suggestions:

A Time for Singing. Published by Augsburg Publishing House, 426 South Fifth Street, Minneapolis, MN 55415. This album of three discs cannot be commended too highly. The 62 hymns are magnificently sung and played. The bargain price is $6.95 with a paperback collection of these hymns (text and full music score) available at 35¢. (One copy accompanies the album.) Not only can an individual or family sing along with these recordings but the total album is also a model of various means of hymn accompaniment and arrangement. Many instruments other than the pipe organ are used. Paul Manz is the organist. Although it is based on the Lutheran hymnbook, most of the hymns are ecumenical in nature. Here are some titles: "Let all mortal flesh keep silence," (M324, L198, P148, RC157) "Jesus shall reign," (B282, M472, L530, P496, RC147) "Crown him with many crowns," (B52, M455, L190, P213, RC63) and "Love divine, all loves excelling." (B58, M283, L315, P399, RC172)

Sing to the Lord—16 Early American Folk Hymns. RCA Victor LSC-2942. The Robert Shaw Chorale. Shaw has several other hymn recordings.

Hymns for All Seasons. EMI Records CSD 3739. King's College Choir, Cambridge, David Willcocks, director.

Hymns from Montreat Music Conference, 1981. Paul Manz, organist. Cassette available through Davis Sound, P.O. Box 240501, Charlotte, NC 28224.

10. *Create a sound film strip on hymns.*□Consider the development of a sound film strip on some aspect or aspects of congregational singing in your church. Some member of your congregation may have the equipment (camera, projector, recorder) to handle the technical matters. The film strip could illustrate the story of a particular hymn or a series of slides could be assembled to show the various images evoked by a nature hymn like "All beautiful the march of days" (M33, P96) or "All creatures of our God and King." (B9, M60, L527, P100, RC8) Here are pictures noted in the latter hymn: sun, moon, wind, clouds, sunrise, sunset, water, fire, earth, flowers, fruit, all persons.

11. *Integrate hymns and the church school curriculum.*□This implies that a hymn task force representative will sit down with the director of Christian education or the church school superintendent or the committee on education and plan a full utilization of the teaching potential of hymns. We are talking here not only of the cognitive but also the affective aspects of learning. Chapter 13 discusses the use of hymnody in the educational program of the local church.

12. *Have a hymn writing project.*□Give your members an opportunity to write hymn texts and tunes. There may be some member who is a specialist in creative writing or who has poetic skills and could help in establishing guidelines for the texts. For

example, would-be writers of hymns might tackle a theme using some of the commonest meters. Common meter has eight syllables in the first line, six in the second, eight in the third, and six in the last. "Our God, our Help in ages past" (B223, M28, L320, P111, RC203) is an example of this meter. Chapters 4 and 6 describe metrical patterns in greater detail. As models, these budding hymnic authors could profitably read hymns by Charles Wesley (1707-1788), Isaac Watts (1674-1748), Brian Wren (1936-), Fred Pratt Green (1903-), and Fred Kaan (1929-). Erik Routley (1917-) in *Hymns Today and Tomorrow* (Abingdon Press, 1964, p. 95) singled out Gilbert Chesterton's (1874-1936) "O God of earth and altar" (M484, L428, P511) as "an excellent example of the modern manner of writing."

Local composers could select one of the new texts just written within the congregation or could find some familiar hymn text in need of a new tune. ("O Love that wilt not let me go" (B368, M234, L324, P400) is an example.) The staff musician might be a helpful critic. Then some of these texts and tunes might be sung at formal or informal occasions by choir and/or congregation.[1]

13. *Schedule regular congregational rehearsals.*☐Congregations need and deserve some specific opportunities to be taught how to sing hymns. This is such an important subject that Chapter 14 is devoted to it.

14. *Include hymn anthems in the choir repertoire.*☐The primary function of the choir is to join with all the other members of the congregation in offering worship to Almighty God and, in so doing, to lead the congregation in worship through hymns, anthems, and in the sung portions of the liturgy. Note that the first responsibility is to lead congregational singing. Chapter 10 describes ways this can be done including using hymn anthems.

15. *Try a hymn cassette program.*☐With the widespread use of cassettes in home and automobile, an imaginative program could be devised to increase hymnic absorption, especially of unfamiliar hymn tunes. For example, several stanzas of each of the different hymns to be sung in public worship for the next three months could be recorded by the choir. These cassettes could be made available to church members for a nominal fee. At the end of this period, they could be returned for transcription of another batch of hymns. Since most laypersons learn new hymns

---

1. See the article "Let the Congregation Compose" by William W. McDermet III in *The Hymn,* January, 1981. p. 30.

by rote, this would enable them to hear the new melodies repeatedly before being asked to sing them. Each of these recorded hymns might be prefaced by a spoken paragraph of information about the text origin, biblical references or tune analysis. It is necessary to secure written permission to record copyright texts and tunes.

16. *Encourage memorization of hymns.*□Encourage persons to memorize hymns. One way would be to print a hymn or at least a stanza in the church bulletin or newsletter with the suggestion that people memorize it. Here is a possible stanza from "How firm a foundation": (B383, M48, L507, P369, RC121)

> Fear not, I am with thee, O be not dismayed,
>   For I am thy God, I will still give thee aid;
> I'll strengthen thee, help thee, and cause thee to stand,
>   Upheld by my righteous, omnipotent hand.

Or, from Bishop Ken's morning hymn "Awake, my soul, and with the sun": (M180, L269, P50)

> Direct, control, suggest, this day,
>   All I design, or do, or say;
> That all my powers, with all their might,
>   In Thy sole glory may unite.

John Calvin wrote: "Now the peculiar gift of men is to sing knowing what he is saying. After the intelligence must follow the heart and the affection, which cannot be unless we have the hymn imprinted on our memory in order never to cease singing."[2] Almost four hundred years later Dietrich Bonhoeffer in *Life Together* said: "A Christian family fellowship will therefore try to master as large as possible a number of hymns that can be sung freely from memory."[3]

17. *Make a favorite hymn survey.*□Interest in hymns and congregational singing can be measurably increased by giving the people a chance to list their ten favorite hymns. These could be collated and the most widely loved hymns could be sung from time to time in public worship with a note that this hymn originated from the survey. After all, the hymns are the music of the

---

2. Translation from Strunk *Source Readings in Music History*, pp. 345-346. (Copyright 1950 by W. W. Norton & Company, Inc. Used by permission).
3. From *Life Together* by Dietrich Bonhoeffer (translated by J. W. Doberstein), p. 81. (Copyright © 1954 by Harper & Row. Used by permission).

people and they should have some democratic way to indicate the ones they would enjoy singing. If this concession is made, they will be much more willing to tackle new hymns. A sound hymnic educational program is based on hard data as to the present knowledge and skill of the group of people. This familiarity survey is one way to determine the present repertoire of your folk.

18. *Introduce variety in hymn singing.*□Some denominations, notably Lutherans, recommend variation of methods of singing hymns. Certain stanzas or entire hymns could be sung in the following ways: unaccompanied, unison, melody-in-tenor, descants, and alternate harmonization. In order that these changes not be considered a surprise or an ambush, they should be introduced discreetly and with due explanation. The bulletin could indicate that certain stanzas will be sung by all the people and other stanzas by choir alone. If desired, men could sing some stanzas and women the others. People on one side of the aisle could answer those across the aisle. The texts and musical structure of hymns give clues to such arrangements.

For example, the hymn "Watchman, tell us of the night" (M358, P149, RC293) is a natural for antiphonal singing between the watchman (soloist or choir) and the travelers (congregation.) The tune *Lasst Uns Erfreuen* (B9, M60, L527, P100, RC8) with its repeated phrases invites antiphonal singing. The first two phrases are identical. Each of the next two phrases contains the same little cascade of four descending steps. (This four-note phrase returns at the end to be repeated five times.) The third phrase is repeated immediately. Thus the over-all pattern is AABBCCBBBBB. The underlined phrases would be the responsive ones with everyone singing the final phrase.

19. *Preach sermons based on hymns.*□Sermons are properly based on the Holy Scriptures. Many of our finest hymns likewise have their roots in God's revealed Word. See, for example, "How firm a foundation" (B383, M48, L507, P369, RC121) which is directly quoted in poetic form mainly from Old Testament sources. Since a great deal of Biblical truth is found in certain hymns, some ministers occasionally preach sermons or give brief talks based on these hymn texts. They thereby accomplish two things: first, they illustrate the Scripture passage which gave birth to the lines of the hymn; and, second, they increase the

comprehension of the congregation whenever that particular hymn is sung. Erik Routley has interpretative essays on forty-nine hymns in his book *Hymns and the Faith* (The Seabury Press, 1956.)

20. *Provide opportunities for informal hymn sings.*□Congregations enjoy informal occasions when they can request their own favorite hymns. Most of the average congregation's hymns are selected for worship occasions by the minister and are usually restricted to three a week. Arrange opportunities when your people can enjoy a wide variety of hymns—maybe several stanzas of each. Granted you will probably receive requests for the most familiar hymns in the book, but you will occasionally be surprised to hear a brand new hymn requested. There is less resistance to tackling a new hymn when it has been requested by one of their own number instead of having it superimposed by the leadership.

From time to time, include some folk songs, rounds, and fun songs.[4]

21. *Teach a class in hymnology.*□A class in the study of hymns and their use has been included in many church continuing education events. Try such a class. In addition to ideas contained in this volume, examine the following three texts designed for congregational study classes:

James Rawlings Sydnor, HYMNS: A CONGREGATIONAL STUDY. Carol Stream, IL: Agape, 1982.
J. Edward Moyer, THE VOICE OF HIS PRAISE: A NEW APPRECIATION OF HYMNODY. Nashville: Graded Press, 1965.
L. David Miller, HYMNS: THE STORY OF CHRISTIAN SONG. Philadelphia: Lutheran Church Press, 1969.

The achievement of great congregational singing is no accident. It is the result of the application of sound educational principles. The employment of any of the 21 suggestions listed above will move a congregation closer to vital, joyous, and sustaining song.

4. For catalog of paperback collections of fun songs, write to World Around Songs, Rt. 5, Box 398, Burnsville, NC 28714.

Chapter II

GREAT CONGREGATIONAL SINGING: WHAT IS IT?

Great congregational singing is being achieved when the entire congregation sings a sizable number of good hymns with spiritual perception and musical artistry. This is the goal toward which every educational effort suggested in this book is directed. If one of the four aspects of this definition is omitted or slighted, the congregation will suffer and the benefits of superior singing will be greatly diminished.

1. *All of the congregation sings.* Everyone in the congregation must be encouraged and educated to sing and to enjoy it. The English composer, William Byrd (c.1542-1623), in the preface to his *Psalms, Sonnets and Songs,* 1588, gave eight reasons for learning to sing and concluded with this couplet:

Since singing is so good a thing
I wish all men would learne to sing.

Many years later, John Wesley (1703-1791) published his famous "Directions for Singing,"[1] the 3rd of which is: "Sing *all*. See that you join with the congregation as frequently as you can. Let not a slight degree of weakness or weariness hinder you. If it is a cross to you, take it up, and you will find it a blessing."

Both of these men were simply reformulating the thought of the psalmist who wrote: "Let the people praise thee, O God; let all the people praise thee." (Ps. 67:3)

Granted that all people are invited to praise God through singing, the fact remains that there are many islands of silence in our Sunday morning congregations where some people just lis-

---

1. *Select Hymns: With Tunes Annext: Designed Chiefly for the Use of the People Called Methodists.* London: Printed in the year 1761.

ten while mainly the choir sings the hymns. Persons have confessed to me that they were told as youngsters that they could not carry a tune and so they have shut up—for scores of years. What a pity! With some of these, I have had opportunity, at their request, to check their tune-carrying ability and frequently have found that they managed to control the pitches of their voice quite well. They were thus launched on a new-found odyssey of enjoying hymn singing. Others may be temporarily restrained from singing because of a sore throat or other physical ailment. I even had a gentleman once apologize to me after a hymn festival for not singing by saying that he had forgotten to bring along his heart pills and thus was afraid to exert himself!

Strive to increase the percentage of people who participate in the singing of hymns. Even if a layperson cannot carry a tune, the Lord accepts the praise. If necessary, a person who cannot or will not sing can participate by opening the hymnal and reading the words while others sing.

2. *The congregation sings a wide variety of good hymns.* The congregation which sings only a dozen or so old favorites can hardly be said to have the quality of singing found in an enterprising congregation which knows a hundred or more excellent hymns. By analogy, persons who are acquainted only with a few contemporary American novelists and *The Readers Digest* will have missed the masterpieces of Shakespeare, Milton, Shelley and other great writers.

Many denominational hymnals contain about 600 hymns. If the congregation sings only about 30 hymns, it is utilizing only five percent of the contents of the hymnal. This is poor stewardship of hymnic resources. The governing board of a local congregation would take a quick hard look at an educational program which employed only five percent of the available rooms in the church school building.

Those of us who know hundreds of superb hymn texts and tunes yearn to transfer them from the printed page into the hearts and lives and voices of our people.

What do we mean by good hymns? This will be explained.

3. *The congregation sings with spiritual perception.* The apostle Paul said, "I will sing with the spirit, and I will sing with the understanding also." (I Corinthians 14:15) The thoughts and emotions contained in the text of a hymn must be understood

and felt by each singer. The music is a vehicle for the expression of these ideas and feelings.

Some leaders think that they have achieved the height of congregational singing when the largest possible volume of sound has issued from the throats of the people. John Wesley was too wise to accept such a shallow test for determining excellence of praise. In the *Minutes of Conference 1746,* he instructed his early Methodist preachers to interrupt a noisy hymn, "by often stopping short and asking the people, 'Now do you know what you said last? Did it suit your case? Did you sing it as to God with the spirit and with the understanding also?' "[2] Imagine the shock on the faces of a staid congregation if the minister would dare interrupt a hymn with questions like these!

Wesley repeated this counsel in the last one of his directions for singing:

"*Above all, sing spiritually.* Have an eye to God in every word you sing. Aim at pleasing him more than yourself, or any other creature. In order to do this, attend strictly to the sense of what you sing, and see that your heart is not carried away with the sound, but offered to God continually; so shall your singing be such as the Lord will approve of here, and reward you when he cometh in the clouds of heaven."

4. *The congregation sings musically.* Good congregational singing is the result of following such simple musical rules as united attack, spirited movement at a tempo set by the organist or pianist, blended firm tone, and vital rhythm. As Sir Walford Davies well said:

> Here we wish to endorse and emphasize the view that congregational singing will never even approach its best until a start is made on the principle that the fundamental principles of choralism should be aimed at in the nave no less than in the choir. Attack, unanimity, vital tone, and rhythm; these call for no degree of skill beyond that attainable by any normally intelligent crowd of adults.[3]

Neither Sir Walford or any other person possessed of common sense would expect a congregation to have the choral finesse

---

2. From *Publications of the Wesley Historical Society, Number 1. John Bennet's Copy of the Minutes of the Conferences of 1744, 1745, 1747, and 1748; with Wesley's Copy of Those for 1746.* London: Wesley Historical Society, 1896. p. 37.
3. From *Music & Worship* by Walford Davies and Harvey Grace. p. 141. New York: The H. W. Gray Company, 1935. Reprinted by AMS Press, New York, NY.

displayed by the Robert Shaw Chorale or any other top choral ensemble. However, many persons have heard large gatherings sing with thrilling musicality.

Wesley had three bits of practical advice for achieving this congregational musicianship:

> *Sing lustily,* and with a good courage. Beware of singing as if you are half-dead or half-asleep; but lift up your voice with strength. Be no more afraid of your voice now, nor more ashamed of its being heard, than when you sing the songs of *Satan.*
>
> *Sing modestly.* Do not bawl, so as to be heard above or distinct from the rest of the congregation—that you may not destroy the harmony—but strive to unite your voices together so as to make one clear melodious sound.
>
> *Sing in time.* Whatever time is sung be sure to keep with it. Do not run before nor stay behind it; but attend close to the leading voices, and move therewith as exactly as you can; and take care not to sing *too slow.* This drawling way naturally steals on all who are lazy; and it is high time to drive it out from among us, and sing all our tunes just as quick as we did at first.[4]

The pilgrimage toward this goal of great congregational singing can and should be a joyful journey. It requires patient and enthusiastic leadership.

---

4. In Wesley's 1761 *Select Hymns,* he added *seven* "Directions for Singing" after the hymns and indexes. He exhorted the reader carefully to observe them in order that "this part of Divine Worship may be the more acceptable to God, as well as the more profitable to himself and others."

The other two directions (1 and 2) which are not quoted in the above text of this chapter are:

1. Learn these tunes before you learn any others; afterwards learn as many as you please.

2. Sing them exactly as they are printed here, without altering or mending them at all; and if you have learned to sing them otherwise, unlearn it as soon as you can.

These seven directions are printed in full at the beginning of the Methodist *The Book of Hymns,* 1964, 1966.

The five directions, included in the body of this chapter, have been printed on a sheet suitable for attaching to flyleaves of hymnals. They can be purchased in quantities from Outlook Publishers, 512 East Main Street, Richmond, VA 23219.

Chapter III

FIVE VALUES OF HYMN SINGING

1. *Through hymn singing, Christians express their feelings and ideas.* Our concept of worship has at its center the priesthood of the individual believer. Therefore, the individual Christian in worship holds converse with his or her Creator and with the fellow worshippers. Many profound feelings and ideas are generated in a true experience of worship. Here are a few examples accompanied by a suggestion of a hymn to express each of them:

—joy in the Christian faith: Charles Wesley's "O for a thousand tongues to sing my great Redeemer's praise" (B69, M1, L559, P141)

—concern for integrity and competence in national political life: Gilbert Chesterton's "O God of earth and altar, bow down and hear our cry; Our earthly rulers falter, Our people drift and die" (M484, L428, P511)

—contrition for personal sins: Synesius' "Lord Jesus, think on me and purge away my sin" (M284, L309, P270, RC167)

—fear and insecurity: "Fear not, I am with you, oh, be not dismayed" from "How firm a foundation" (B383, M48, L507, P369, RC121)

—gratitude for God's sustenance: Martin Rinkart's "Now thank we all our God with hearts and hands and voices" (B234, M49, L533, P9, RC189)

—despair: Martin Luther's "Out of the depths I cry to you." (M526, L295, RC224)

These emotions and concepts can frequently be better understood, interpreted, verbalized, and accepted if they have been expressed or articulated in a hymn. This provision of a vocabu-

16

lary for prayer was described by a Scottish Presbyterian, George S. Stewart, in reference to the value and use of books of prayer. He wrote, "I find them often helpful in giving the word or phrase which gathers up most fitly what is in my heart and deepens its meaning. The power of the right word in purifying and strengthening prayer is very great."[1]

This same idea was expressed by Brian Wren as he commented on a hymn stanza written by Fred Kaan. Kaan's hymn "Lord, as we rise to leave this shell of worship" (E87) has in it the following stanza:

> Give us an eye for openings to serve you;
> make us alert when calm is interrupted,
> ready and wise to use the unexpected:
> sharpen our insight.

"Most of us," says Wren, "when we look back on a week, can recall occasions when calm was interrupted, or the unexpected disrupted our plans, and the memories are often a cause for confession. But by placing these words in a hymn, the author invites us to anticipate these occasions, and perhaps better prepare for them. Few of us could think such thoughts as clearly if we had not been helped by the words of the hymn."[2]

2. *Through hymn singing, Christians can tell others what they believe.* John and Charles Wesley learned about the solid faith of the Moravians as they listened to their singing aboard the little ship Simmonds on January 25, 1736. They were on a voyage to Savannah, Georgia, when a tempest overtook the ship. At seven o'clock that evening they attended a vesper service of these Moravians. John described what happened:

> In the midst of the psalm wherewith their service began, wherein we were mentioning the power of God, the sea broke over, split the mainsail in pieces, covered the ship, and poured in between the decks, as if the great deep had already swallowed us up. A terrible screaming began among the English. The Germans looked up, and without interruption calmly sang on. I asked one of them afterwards, 'Were you not afraid?' He answered, 'I thank God, no.' I

---

1. From *The Lower Levels of Prayer,* pp. 119-120. Nashville: Abingdon Press, 1939.
2. From "The Challenge of the Words" in a symposium "The Hymn Today." Reproduced with permission from the Bulletin of the Hymn Society of Great Britain and Ireland, January 1977.

asked, 'But were not your women and children afraid?' He replied
mildly, 'No, our women and children were not afraid to die.'[3]

This frightening experience, wherein the Moravians expressed their calm faith by their singing, inaugurated a life-long
friendship with these Christians. Two years later at Moravian
meetings at Aldersgate in London, these brothers experienced
conversions within four days of each other. From these encoun-
ters the Wesleys went out into the fruitful ministry which
helped transform the heart of England.

Two centuries before the Wesleys had this ocean tempest experience, John Calvin arrived in Geneva. He found that there
was no tradition of congregational singing. He wrote in 1537
that he desired to have the psalms sung in the churches but he
said, "We are unable to compute the profit and edification which
will arise from this, except after having experimented."[4] One
year later the city council exiled him. He went down the Rhine
river to Strasbourg where he frequently heard the stirring singing in Martin Bucer's congregation. When Calvin returned to
Geneva several years later, he wrote the following words in the
preface to his 1542 psalter: "In truth we know by experience that
song has great force and vigor to move and inflame the hearts of
men to invoke and praise God with a more vehement and ardent
zeal."[5] Bucer's people had convinced him.[6]

People are attracted by music because the love of tonal beauty
is at the heart of all human beings. When genuine texts are set
to strong melodies and are sung with real feeling, the effect on
participants and listeners is powerful. It is one of the most obvious ways of extending the Christian faith. Hymns have therefore always been a powerful adjunct to the mission enterprise.

3. *Through hymn singing, Christians are bound in closer fellowship.* Some psychologists believe that collections of people

---

3. From *The Journal of the Rev. John Wesley, A.M.*, edited by Nehemiah Curnock, Vol.
   I, pp. 142-143. London: Epworth Press, 1938.
4. From *Calvin: Theological Treatises* in *The Library of Christian Classics.* Vol. XXII,
   pp. 53-54. Philadelphia: The Westminster Press, 1954.
5. From *Source Readings in Music History* by Oliver Strunk. The entire preface is
   found on pages 345-348. (Copyright © 1950 by W. W. Norton & Company, Inc. Used
   by permission.)
6. For description of Bucer's views on congregational singing, see Bard Thompson,
   Liturgies of the Western Church, pp. 159-166. Cleveland: The World Publishing
   Company, 1962.

remain individuals until a single event or purpose or emotion molds them into groups, and that then the group lives, feels, and thinks in a way of its own, superior in energy and intensity to the activity of any of its members.

When a group of Christians sings with vitality the same melody, responds to identical rhythms, thinks and feels the same ideas and emotions during the act of common praise, it becomes well-nigh inevitable that each is drawn closer in spirit to his or her neighbor. They cease to be isolated individuals. They become more completely members of the body of Christ. As Bonhoeffer wrote, "It is the voice of the Church that is heard in singing together. It is not you that sings, it is the Church that is singing, and you, as a member of the Church, may share in its song. Thus all singing together that is right must serve to widen our spiritual horizon, make us see our little company as a member of the great Christian Church on earth, and help us willingly and gladly to join our singing, be it feeble or good, to the song of the Church."[7]

In 1966 President Donald Shriver of Union Theological Seminary in New York City attended a world gathering of Christians in Geneva. He described the experience as follows:

> When almost any group of human beings from seventy countries comes together, one expects tension, verbal fireworks, and tempers. The conference had these things, yet from the beginning it had an underlying unity which almost defied analysis. This was immediately apparent in conference worship. Indeed, on the opening day, this Presbyterian's heart skipped a beat when "Old Hundredth" broke forth from the assembly with an electric enthusiasm impossible to forget. It was the right hymn sung in the right place in the right way. Here in Geneva, four hundred years ago, the words had been written by an English exile, William Kethe. Here also the tune was composed by Calvin's master of the choristers, Louis Bourgeois. And here in the very streets, with many such metrical psalms, the Genevans had 'roared aloud' their joy in the Lord. Such a joyful noise the World Conference on Church and Society reproduced on that Tuesday afternoon in July, 1966.

The hymn was "All people that on earth do dwell." (B17, M21, L245, P24, E21, RC14) The service closed with "O God of earth and altar." (M484, L428, P511) Shriver concluded:

---

7. From *Life Together* by Dietrich Bonhoeffer (translated by J. W. Doberstein), p. 81. (Copyright © 1954 by Harper & Row. Used by permission.)

> Communists and capitalists, revolutionaries and conservatives,
> black robed orthodox bishops and sari clad Indian housewives,
> American business men and African politicians—when all these
> can sing such words in the way they sang them, few present could
> have doubted the reality of the world church.[8]

This conference, incidentally, sang undoubtedly from *Cantate Domino,* a polyglot hymnal published by the World Council of Churches. The hymns in this book, as do the hymns in most hymnals, originate from Christians of various denominations in many countries and from many centuries. So the unifying power of hymns brings Christians closer to the members of the immediate congregation. It helps them feel a community of spirit with Christians of various creeds, nations, and races. Finally, it leads them into fellowship with the redeemed who lived long ago.

4. *Through hymn singing, Christians are instructed in the fundamentals of their faith.* Albert van den Heuvel in the preface to *Risk: New Hymns for a New Day* wrote:

> It is the hymns, repeated over and over again, which form the
> container of much of our faith. They are probably in our age the
> only confessional documents which we learn by heart. As such they
> have taken the place of our catechisms. Moreover many traditions
> are demonstrably determined by their hymnals. Think of the Or-
> thodox Churches, the Methodist, the Salvation Army and the Re-
> formed (Psalms.) There is ample literature about the great forma-
> tive influence of the hymns of a tradition on its members. Tell me
> what you sing, and I'll tell you who you are![9]

The hymnal could be called a commentary on the Holy Scriptures and on Christian experience. Almost every facet of our faith has been expressed through hymns. A glance at the Table of Contents and at the Topical Index of any major hymnal will demonstrate the validity of this statement.

Here are two examples of hymns which are explicitly doctrinal. Cyril Alington (1872-1955), former chaplain to the British crown, wrote a hymn "Come, ye people, rise and sing" (P39)

---

8. From Donald R. Shriver, "Now We Know Our Neighbor." Sept. 26, 1966 issue of *The Presbyterian Outlook*. Used by permission of The Presbyterian Outlook, 512 E. Main St., Richmond, VA 23219.

9. From Vol. II, Number 3, (Copyright © 1966 by World Council of Churches. Used by permission).

which has three stanzas defining the attributes of the Three
Persons of the Trinity. Here is the stanza addressed to Jesus
Christ:

> Praise we God the only Son, who in mercy sought us;
> Born to save a world undone, out of death He brought us;
> Here awhile he showed His love, suffered uncomplaining,
> Now He pleads for us above, risen, ascended, reigning!

Samuel Stone (1839-1900) based his familiar hymn "The
Church's one foundation" (B236, M297, L369, P437, RC262) on
the ninth article in the Apostles' Creed, "I believe in . . . the Holy
Catholic Church." Sung attentively, this text will unfold to the
singer a comprehensive picture of the Body of Christ, the Christian Church.

Many other hymns instruct by implication. For example,
Synesius of Cyrene (c. 375-430) testifies that he believed that
Jesus Christ was alive in the fifth century and could hear his
prayers. He said so in his hymn which is in many of our hymnals:

> Lord Jesus, think on me
> And purge away my sin;
> From selfish passions set me free
> And make me pure within.
> (M284, L309, P270, RC167)

5. *Through hymns, Christians are sustained in daily
life.* The preceding four values are realized mainly in hymn
singing during public worship. However, countless believers
find their spirits buoyed and strengthened as they recollect the
words and tunes of their memorized hymns. The Moravians
especially have valued the daily use of hymns. On June 17, 1722,
a little group of Christians came to the estate of Count Nicholas
Ludwig von Zinzendorf (1700-1760) in Saxony, Germany. They
were spiritual and lineal descendants of the sturdy founders of
the ancient Unitas Fratrum, established March 1, 1457. To encourage these Moravians, the Count would select a Scripture
passage or two and a hymn verse or stanza and each day announce them to these Christians. The Moravians have maintained this custom and publish an annual booklet *Daily Watch-
words being Scripture Texts with Appropriate Hymn-verses and*

Prayers for Every Day of the Year (Moravian Church, Northern Province, 5 Market Street, Bethlehem, Pennsylvania 18018.)

The German theologian, Dietrich Bonhoeffer, found his terminal days in the Nazi prison more bearable because of hymns. He wrote to his parents, "What a great comfort Paul Gerhardt's hymns are! I am learning them off by heart."[10] One of these Gerhardt hymns could have been the following:

> Give to the winds thy fears;
> Hope and be undismayed;
> God hears thy sighs and counts thy tears,
> God shall lift up thy head.
>
> (B224, M51, P364)

---

10. From *Letters and Papers from Prison*. Edited by Eberhard Bethge. Translated by Reginald H. Fuller. p. 28. London: SCM Press, 1953.

Chapter IV

THE HYMN: ITS WORDS AND MUSIC

In corporate worship and in daily life, hymns can have a profound, sustaining, and complex effect on a person. Therefore, leaders who are interested in improving congregational singing should spend some time pondering the means whereby hymn reading and hymn singing can shape the faith and influence the daily lives of their congregational members. This chapter is designed to stimulate this process of reflection.

A. An Introduction to the Hymn.

The effect of hymns is rendered more complex and powerful because two languages are employed—words and music. Each of these arts adds a dimension to the impression and expression of hymns. Emil Brunner, the Swiss theologian, explains this interaction:

> The message of what God has done for our redemption certainly cannot be expressed as music, and what God wills to say to us in Jesus Christ cannot be painted. In this respect the human word is not simply one method among others, for human speech alone can indicate quite unambiguously God's thought, will, and work. But music can very well support the word of the proclamation as an expression of the feeling aroused by the Word, and the art of painting may suggest in a pictorial manner what the Word means. This is no small service, and the truly great Christian artists have never wished it otherwise.[1]

1. From *The Divine Imperative*, p. 502. (Copyright © 1947 by Lutterworth Press. Used by permission).

The Purpose of Hymns

We can understand the basic purpose of hymns if we consider first the purpose of art in general. Leo Tolstoy (1828–1910) in 1898 published a little book entitled *What Is Art?* He sums up his answer in one sentence: "To evoke in oneself a feeling one has once experienced and having evoked it in oneself then by means of movements, lines, colours, sounds, or forms expressed in words, so to transmit that feeling that others experience the same feeling—this is the activity of art."[2]

The purpose of hymns is also to enable as many Christians as possible to identify with the faith experiences, to enjoy the spiritual insights, to experience the sustaining reality of God's love which belonged to hymn writers and which are expressed in the words and music of their great hymns. When Dietrich Bonhoeffer (1906–1945) was in solitary confinement in the Nazi Tegel prison in Berlin, he wrote, "During this time Paul Gerhardt was a wonderful help, more than I could have dreamed of."[3] Paul Gerhardt (1606–1676) had been dead for over 250 years and yet through his hymns he enabled this isolated Christian to experience the presence of the love of God revealed in Jesus Christ. This Gerhardt stanza was undoubtedly one of his favorites:

> Since Jesus is my Friend and I to Him belong,
> It matters not what foes intend however fierce and strong.
>
> (P218)

Quality in Hymns

The final arbiter of greatness in a hymn is the test of long, satisfactory use by the Church. In C. S. Phillips' words, "Time, on the whole, is a sound critic in hymnody as in other matters; those hymns survive that deserve to survive."[4] The next chapter "A Chronological Ecumenical List of Basic Hymns" contains 227 titles, the large majority of which are excellent hymns.

Granted that the average person in the pew may give little

2. From *What is Art? and Essays in Art*, p. 123. Translated by Aylmer Maude. London: Oxford University Press, 1930.
3. From *Letters and Papers from Prison*, p. 64. Edited by Eberhard Bethge. Translated by Reginald H. Fuller. London: SCM Press, 1953.
4. From *Hymnody Past and Present*, p. 249. London: S.P.C.K., 1937.

thought to the question of what is a good, mediocre, or bad hymn, it behooves worship and educational leaders in the local church (as well as hymnal editors) to have some idea of what constitutes excellence in hymns. Here is a list a dozen hymns which in my opinion contain words and music, well matched, that exemplify my ideals of great hymns:

A mighty Fortress is our God (B37, M20, L228, P91, E25, RC2,3)	*Ein Feste Burg*
All creatures of our God and King (B9, M60, L527, P100, RC8)	*Lasst Uns Erfreuen*
All people that on earth do dwell (B17, M21, L245, P24, RC14)	*Old Hundredth*
God moves in a mysterious way (B439, M215, L483, P112)	*Neumark*
If thou but suffer God to guide thee (B203, M210, L453, P344)	*Picardy*
Let all mortal flesh keep silence (M324, L198, P148, RC157)	*Nun Danket*
Now thank we all our God (B234, M49, L533, P9, RC189)	*Dundee*
O God of earth and altar (M484, L428, P511)	*Llangloffan*
O love, how deep, how broad, how high (L88)	*Deo Gracias*
Of the Father's love begotten (B62, M357, L42, P7, RC216)	*Divinum Mysterium*
Rejoice, ye pure in heart (E48)	*Vineyard Haven*
The King of love my Shepherd is (L456, P106, RC268)	*St. Columba*

A Comprehensive Theology in Hymns

A Christian congregation needs a balanced hymnic diet just as it should have a comprehensive exposition of the Bible. Whether it *can* be fed such a diet depends, first, on the editors of its hymnal; next, whether it *will* be fed such a diet depends on the week by week choices of the pastor and the educational leaders. Most denominational hymnals are beginning now to offer a cafeteria of hymns from which a balanced menu of hymns can be selected.

What do we mean by a balanced hymnic diet? From the textual standpoint we mean a hymnody which expresses the entire spectrum of Christian doctrine, experience, and obligation. About a century ago the Scottish mystic, George Matheson, described the unevenness of hymns in his day. He wrote:

> To my mind they have one great defect; they lack humanitarianism. There is any amount of doctrine in the Trinity, Baptism, Atonement, or the Christian life as such, but what of the secular life—the infirmary, the hospital, the home of refuge? . . . I don't think our hymns will ever be what they ought to be, until we get them inspired by a sense of the enthusiasm of, and for, humanity. It is rather a theological point, perhaps, but the hymnists speak of the surrender to Christ. They forget that Christ is not simply an individual. He is Head of a body, the body of humanity; and it no longer expresses the idea correctly to join yourself to Christ only, you must give yourself to the whole brotherhood of man to fulfill the idea.[5]

This analysis is all the more impressive when we recall that this blind Scot gave us two hymns of deep inner experience: "Make me a captive, Lord" (M184, P308) and "O Love, that wilt not let me go." (B368, M234, L324, P400)

This imbalance is being corrected in contemporary hymns and hymnals. An examination of the table of contents and the actual hymns in many new books demonstrates this. Contrast Matheson's lament with Olle Engström's introduction to Fred Kaan's *Songs and Hymns from Sweden:*

> A common factor from country to country is the renewal in patterns of worship caused by the immense changes in the society in which the churches have to carry out their task . . . characteristic of the new texts is that they are not abstract systematic theology in rhyme, as was so often the case in the past. They proclaim the presence of God in the Living Christ and the Spirit in the everyday life of men and women—even in the cities. There are more pavements, there is more smell of hectic rush hours than ever before in Christian hymnbooks, where the only city that was mentioned was the heavenly Jerusalem. The troubled hearts of men and women in this era of frustration—and God's concern not only for uncertain

5. Donald Macmillan, *The Life of George Matheson*, p. 185. New York: A. C. Armstrong and Son, 1907.

and desolate individuals but for the whole of creation . . . these are
among the main themes that occur.[6]

Consider the immense recent changes in our society, referred
to by Engström: World War II, the beginning of the atomic age,
the Supreme Court desegration decision of 1954, the civil rights
march on Selma, Alabama, the rebellion of youth against the
establishment, the wars in Korea and Vietnam, concern for the
third world, the mid-east tensions, the development of liberation
theology, energy shortages, inflation. Such developments have
compelled hymn writers to address many of these issues and
their implications in the light of the Christian gospel.

Some of these new hymns contain general calls to social service. For example, Albert F. Bayly (1901-) wrote "Lord, Whose
Love through Humble Service" (M479, L423) in 1961. It is a
remarkable comprehensive text calling for divine help for mo-
tive and power to serve all people:

> Still your children wander homeless; Still the hungry cry for bread;
> Still the captives long for freedom; Still in grief we mourn our dead;
> As you, Lord, in deep compassion Healed the sick and freed the soul,
> By your Spirit send your power To our world to make it whole.[7]

"O God, Empower Us to Stem the Hatreds that Divide" (L422)
by Lee M. Baldwin (1906-) is a prayer for wisdom in interper-
sonal relationships:

> When neighbors feel distress, or grieve, Or sickness takes its toll,
> Enable us to feel their pain, The better to console.
> And when the neighbor's path is dark And heavy with despair,
> Help us to lift the Gospel's light And show the Father's care.[8]

"O Holy City, Seen of John" (M481, P508, RC204), written in
1909 by Walter Russell Bowie (1882-1969), contains this powerful stanza:

6. Copyright © 1976 by Stainer & Bell, Ltd. All rights reserved. Used by Permission of
   Galaxy Music Corp., N.Y. sole U.S. agent.
7. Words from "Seven New Social Welfare Hymns" copyright 1961 by the Hymn Society of America. Used by permission.
8. Text copyright 1976 by Lee McCullough Baldwin.

"O shame to us who rest content while lust and greed for gain
In street and shop and tenement wring gold from human pain,
And bitter lips in blind despair cry, "Christ hath died in vain.""[9]

Erik Routley's (1917–) hymn "All who love and serve your city" (L436, E54, 55) seems destined to take a permanent place in ecumenical hymnody.

The necessity for preserving our environment is written into the texts of many new hymns. Brian Wren (1936–) has a hymn whose first stanza is:

Thank you, Lord, for water, soil and air—
Large gifts supporting every thing that lives.
Forgive our spoiling and abuse of them,
Help us renew the face of the earth. (E78)[10]

Another ecological hymn is "God in His Love for Us Lent Us This Planet" (E75) by F. Pratt Green (1903–).

Long have the wars of man ruined his harvest;
Long has Earth bowed to the terror of force,
Now we pollute it, in cynical silence:
Poison the fountain of life at its source.

Casual despoilers, or high priests of Mammon
Selling the future for present rewards,
Careless of life and contemptuous of beauty:
Bid us remember; the Earth is the Lord's![11]

Fred Kaan (1929–) addresses the problem of hunger and plenty in the hymn "Now join we to praise the creator" (E92, RC187) with such words as "we cry for the plight of the hungry while harvests are left in the field, for orchards neglected and wanting, for produce from markets withheld."[12]

The danger of focusing our hymnody mainly on the inner life was expressed by Martin Marty who wrote regarding Christian people, "Isolate them from the moral and ethical dimensions of

9. Words from *Hymns of the Kingdom of God.* Coffin and Vernon, Copyright 1910 by Harper & Brothers, publishers.
10. Copyright © 1973 by Hope Publishing Company. Used by permission.
11. Words from *Sixteen Stewardship Hymns of the Environment,* Copyright by The Hymn Society of America. Used by permission.
12. Words copyright 1968 by Galliard Ltd. All rights reserved.

Christian life, and you have church life in a hall of mirrors, a setting for self-seeking and narcissism."[13]

Singability of Hymns

When is a hymn tune congregational and when is it choral? Presumably this is an underlying question in the minds of all hymnal editors because there is a limit of complexity beyond which a group of musical amateurs cannot go without extensive training and rehearsal. Therefore these editors of hymnals select hymns and especially hymn tunes which can be mastered by the average congregation.

Any skillful church musician who is sensitive to congregational singing abilities can rank hymn tunes according to difficulty or ease of learning. For example, *Nicaea* "Holy, Holy, Holy, Lord God Almighty" (B1, M26, L165, P11) is much easier to teach a congregation than the tune *King's Weston* "At the name of Jesus" (B363, M76, L179, P143).

Try ranking the following five tunes in order of ease of learning by your congregation. Which one could they learn quickest and with which one would they have the most difficulty?

Geneva (M124, L437, P512, RC77)
Beecher (B3, M283, P399)
Ebenezer (B340, M242, L233, P361, RC280)
Bryn Calfaria (B121, M364, L156, P90)
Forest Green (B154, M33, P96)

It behooves ministers and musicians, who are beginning an exploration of the hymnal with their people, to learn to identify and introduce those melodies first which can be absorbed without an undue amount of training.

Motives for Writing Hymns

The themes and content of hymns are determined by the motives of the hymn writers. Charles Wesley wrote "O for a thousand tongues" (B69, M1, L559, P141) to celebrate the first

---

13. From an article "New Patterns for a New Age" in *Church Music,* Issue 67-2, p. 3. Published by Concordia Publishing House, St. Louis, MO.

anniversary of his conversion on May 21, 1738. The hymn "All beautiful the march of days" (M33, P96) was written by Frances Witmarsh Wile in response to a request by a hymnal editor for a "winter" hymn. In 1954 the World Council of Churches, meeting in Evanston, Illinois, had as its theme "Christ, the Hope of the World." In preparation for this meeting, The Hymn Society of America invited hymn writers to submit texts based on this topic. From more than 500 new texts, the committee selected Georgia Harkness' hymn "Hope of the world, Thou Christ of great compassion" (B364, M161, L493, P291) as the assembly theme hymn.

Fred Kaan describes how he happened to write a Communion Calypso "Let us talents and tongues employ" (C7):

> Normally, I suppose the text of the hymn is born before its melody. The hymn writer may work to a certain meter and rhythm but the choice of the tune or the composition of the music comes later. Not so with this one. Jamaican-born Doreen Potter was a near neighbor of ours in Geneva. She came to me one day with this bouncing melody, largely based on a Jamaican folk song, and I decided on the spot to write a text for it that might help capture a mood of celebration at the eucharist. You see, communion tends so often to be a solemn affair in our churches and rightly so, for it brings to mind the supreme sacrifice in human history—but it is also given to us as an opening for celebration and opportunity for anticipating the unity of all people around a festive table. Its first major airing was at the assembly of the World Council of Churches in Nairobi where we not only sang it but we danced it accompanied by a pop group and loud clapping.[14]

Hymn tune composers likewise have myriad motives. The Hymn Society of America has issued an invitation to composers to write new music for 22 well-known hymn texts such as "Dear Lord and Father of mankind," (B270, M235, L506, P416) "The Church's one foundation," (B236, M297, L369, P437, RC262) and "Jesus calls us: o'er the tumult." (B367, M107, L494, P269) Dr. Richard Wetzel (1935–) was commissioned to provide music for W. H. Auden's "He is the Way." (E72) His beautiful and flexible melody is called *New Dance*. In writing the powerful melody *Sine Nomine* for his 1906 *The English Hymnal*, Dr. Ralph

---

14. Narrated by Fred Kaan in the cassette based on Carlton Young's *Choirbook for Saints and Singers.* Agape issued the cassette under the code number 938. (Copyright © 1980 by Agape. Used by permission.)

Vaughan Williams undoubtedly felt that "For all the saints" (B144, M536, L174, P425, RC80) needed a new setting.

B. Hymn Texts

The subject matter of hymns is as wide as Christian faith and experience. It far exceeds the classic limitations placed on it by St. Augustine in his commentary on Psalm 148 where he wrote that hymns were "songs with praise to God." Granted that hymns of praise and prayer are central in our hymnals, we have many hymns whose subjects are not praise of God but which enable us to obey Paul's injunction to teach and admonish one another "in psalms and hymns and spiritual songs."[15] Here are several examples: "Come, labor on, who dares stand idle?" (P287) and "O come, all ye faithful." (B81, M386, L45, P170, RC193) We also have hymns addressed to ourselves such as "Awake, my soul, stretch every nerve" (M249, P346) and "Bless, O my soul! the living God." (P8)

For a description of a model hymn, here is Dr. Millar Patrick's definition:

> ... he [Isaac Watts] set forever the example of what the congregational hymn should be. What made his own hymns so popular was their fidelity to Scripture, their consistent objectivity and freedom from introspection, and their exact suitability, in ideas and in the limpid clearness of their language, for giving voice to the religious thought and emotion of the average believer; these qualities make his best hymns perfect for the expression of a congregation's worship. He showed also that a good hymn for popular use should have a single theme, organic unity, boldness of attack in the opening line, and a definite progression of thought throughout to a marked and decisive climax. Also, it should be short. His hymns are brief, compact, direct, and telling. Reasons like these justified James Montgomery in saying that Watts was "the real founder of English hymnody."[16]

From this definition we shall select four salient points for amplification: (1) Scriptural fidelity, (2) spiritual reality and wholesomeness, (3) simplicity and beauty, and (4) structural

---

15. Colossians 3:16.
16. From *The Story of the Church's Song*, pp. 131–132. Copyright © M. E. Bratcher, 1962. Richmond: John Knox Press. Used by permission.

soundness. To this we add a fifth point, the need for inclusive language.

1. Scriptural Fidelity

Christian hymns have their roots in the Holy Bible. The metrical psalms are poetic versions of the book of Psalms ("All people that on earth do dwell" (B17, M21, L245, P24, RC14) is based on Psalm 100.) "How firm a foundation" (B383, M48, L507, P369, RC121) is based so solidly on various passages of Scripture that most of the stanzas are in quotation marks. The Scots extended the scope of their congregational song by versifying passages in the New Testament. Matthew's account of the institution of the Lord's Supper (26:26–29) is paraphrased as "'Twas on that night, when doom'd to know." (P448) Some stanzas from their paraphrase of the Song of Simeon (Nunc Dimittis, Luke 2:25–33) are sung by congregations at the conclusion of Holy Communion after the manner established by John Calvin in Geneva:

> Now, Lord! according to thy word,
>   let me in peace depart;
> Mine eyes have thy salvation seen,
>   and gladness fills my heart.
>
> This great salvation, long prepar'd,
>   and now disclos'd to view,
> Hath prov'd thy love was constant still,
>   and promises were true.
>
> That Sun I now behold, whose light
>   shall heathen darkness chase,
> And rays of brightest glory pour
>   around thy chosen race.
>
> To Father, Son, and Holy Ghost,
>   the God whom we adore,
> Be glory, as it was, and is,
>   and shall be evermore.[17] (Tune: *DUNDEE*)

Many other hymns contain a generous amount of explicit reference to Scripture. "Where cross the crowded ways of life" (B311, M204, L429, P507) is rooted in these Biblical passages: Matthew 9:36, 10:42 and Revelation 21:2.

17. From *The Scottish Psalter 1929.* p. 215. London: Oxford University Press, 1929.

2. Spiritual Reality and Wholesomeness

The hymn must come from the heart of the writer if it is to move the heart of the singer. There must be an experience of spiritual reality at the source. John Drinkwater has written that "contact with fine poetry is precisely contact with the most vital and personal experience conveyed to us in the most persuasive medium invented by man ... pregnant and living words."[18]

To Martin Luther, God was a mighty Fortress. To him life was a struggle whose outcome was sure—"And He must win the battle.... His Kingdom is forever." The object of this immortal hymn is to rouse our dormant faith and to nerve us with the spiritual energy and fortitude of the German Reformer. One has only to read the following lines of the blind Scotsman, George Matheson, to catch the devotion in his heart:

> Make me a captive, Lord,
> And then I shall be free;
> Force me to render up my sword,
> And I shall conquerer be.
>
> I sink in life's alarms
> When by myself I stand;
> Imprison me within Thine arms,
> And strong shall be my hand. (M184, P308)

We must keenly scrutinize hymns in current use to determine whether they have positive values and wholesome influences. Especially should we be alert lest our hymns induce sentimentality in our people. Here is Erik Routley's definition: "I define 'sentimentality' as the evocation or the seeking of emotional satisfaction divorced from reason and responsibility."[19]

3. Simplicity and Beauty

The act of hymn singing provides little opportunity for leisurely reflection on the text. When singing "For all the saints" (B144, M536, L174, P425, RC80) to Vaughan Williams' tune *Sine Nomine,* most of the syllables flit through the consciousness

18. From *The Muse in Council, Being Essays on Poets and Poetry,* p. 60. Boston: Houghton Mifflin Company, 1925.
19. Article "The Vocabulary of Church Music" in *Union Seminary Quarterly Review,* Vol. XVIII, No. 2. January 1963, p. 142. New York, NY. (Copyright © 1963 by Union Theological Seminary in the City of New York. Used by permission.)

at the rate of two per second. Furthermore, congregations include persons of many degrees of cultural and intellectual
achievement. Hymn meanings must therefore be readily apparent. High-flown allusions, involved structure, or long, unfamiliar words reduce comprehension.

In the original preface to Isaac Watts' hymns, he stated that
he "endeavored to make the sense plain and obvious ... I have
cut out the lines that are too sonorous ... lest a more exalted
Turn of Thought or Language should darken or disturb the Devotion of the plainest Souls."

This statement should not be construed to mean that the
beauty of true poetry cannot be present in hymns. Indeed, the
kindling of the imagination through an exact turn of word or
phrase can illumine the mind with an unforgettable spiritual
truth. Inveterate readers of hymn texts can recall scores of
beautiful lines or stanzas which they have stored in memory,
such as:

—"His spirit floweth free, high surging where it will ...
   (from "The God of Abraham praise") (B25, L544, P89, RC230)

—"All beautiful the march of days,
As seasons come and go;
The Hand that shaped the rose hath wrought
The crystal of the snow ... " (M33, P96)

—"Who trusts in God's unchanging love
Builds on the rock that nought can move ... "
   (from "If thou but suffer God to guide thee.") (B203, M210, L453, P344)

4. Structural Soundness

Single theme, organic unity, boldness of attack in the opening
line, definite progression of thought throughout to a marked and
decisive climax, brevity—the presence of these qualities will
give a hymn architectural soundness. These characteristics are
exemplified in the better hymns of Isaac Watts and Charles
Wesley.

There are many patterns which give organic unity to hymns.
Some are based on the Trinity, with stanzas devoted to the at-
tributes of each Person of the Godhead ("Come, Thou Almighty
King," (B2, M3, L522, P244, RC55) "Ancient of Days," (M459,
P246) and "Come, ye people, rise and sing.") (P39) Other exam-

ples are two hymns based on Jesus' words, "I am the way, the truth, and the life." ("Thou art the Way; to Thee alone") (M75, P22, RC278) and "He is the Way.") (E72) Georgia Harkness' hymn "Hope of the world" (B364, M161, L493, P291) depicts in the various stanzas the development of the life and mission of Jesus. Henry Hallam Tweedy's hymn "Eternal God, whose power upholds" (M476, P485, RC72) describes stanza by stanza the God of love, truth, beauty, and righteousness and grace.

5. The Need for Inclusive Language

The impact of the women's rights movement in regard to hymnody is in the increasing use of inclusive language in texts sung in public worship. An example of official denominational action in this direction is found in a decision of the General Assembly of the United Presbyterian Church in the United States of America. This governing body in 1971 directed:

> That since the so-called generic usages of masculine nouns, pronouns, and adjectives are no longer acceptable in any church documents. in all new church documents the generic use of masculine nouns, pronouns, and adjectives shall be replaced by one of the following: (1) the woman-man or she-he format or formula to include all forms. (2) the use of plural pronouns and nouns to replace the masculine singular, and (3) the use of other appropriate nouns, pronouns, and adjectives which include both sexes. That all present church documents be revised in the next three years in accordance with the same principle. (*Minutes,* Part 1, 1971, p. 313)

The National Council of Church of Christ in America has taken a similar action.

The *Lutheran Book of Worship*'s editors worked hard to find solutions to this problem. In the introductory volume *Lutherans at Worship*[20] we find this principle: "Each [hymn] had to avoid sexist and racist references and imagery, including anti-Semitic inferences." Let us examine several examples of their efforts.

"He who would valiant be" (L498) by John Bunyan (1628–1688) has been changed to "*All* who would valiant be 'gainst all disaster, Let *them* in constancy follow the master. There's no discouragement shall make *them* once relent *their* first avowed intent to be *true* pilgrims."

---

20. Stauffer, Doan, and Aune, p. 89. (Copyright © 1978 Augsburg Publishing House.)

But, when they came to William Pierson Merrill's "Rise up, O men of God," (B268, M174, P352) they wisely and completely abandoned his text except for a slight resemblance in the title. Their new text is "Rise up, O saints of God." (LBW383)

Hymnal editors together with hymn and anthem writers should give serious heed to James R. White who writes: "No longer do we have a choice to be concerned or not about sexist language. A fundamental issue of justice is involved, and the church cannot be silent in matters of justice without being a disobedient church . . . We must move to language that affirms both women and men."[21]

C. Hymn Music

A hymn tune is a musical form of sufficient simplicity and appeal that it can be sung without rehearsal by a congregation of musical amateurs. The requisite qualification for composing enduring hymn tunes was well stated by Erik Routley:

> Writing music for unmusical people to sing actually amounts to composing folk songs; and it is not surprising to discover how many successful hymn tunes have been composed by ministers of religion. They knew what it was like to stand in a pew and sing. Organists have done it admirably when they too had this remembrance. The person who cannot compose what ordinary people can sing is the musician who, while excellent in any other musical respect, has forgotten or never knew what hymn singing is like for the singer.[22]

Proof of this statement can be seen by studying the hymns listed in Chapter 5 to determine which are the most popular. Then analyze the tunes of these most popular hymns. In almost every case you will discover skillfull repetition of themes and the singability of folk music.

A hymn tune is a living organism as it is being sung, and its effects are complex. Simultaneously we are influenced by the shape of the melody, the particular chord, the duration of the tone, and the location of this tone within the phrase and entire

21. From "The Words of Worship: Beyond Liturgical Sexism." *The Christian Century,* December 13, 1978, pp. 1202, 1206.
22. *Church Music and the Christian Faith,* p. 90. Carol Stream, Ill.: (Copyright © by Agape, 1978. Used by permission.)

melody. In analyzing the components of a good hymn tune, we should consider them under four headings: Melody, Harmony, Rhythm (time measurement) and Structure.

1. Melody

The prescription for a beautiful, noble, enduring hymn melody is almost impossible to put in words. The British Archbishops' Committee said this:

> Melody can depict both strength and grace, and among the factors to be taken into account these three may be specially noted: (1) advance by steps of a second; (2) euphony in the larger intervals; and (3) arpeggio movement through common chords. These three, in a gracious but vital blend, should never fail to produce a fitting church melody.[23]

As an example Vaughan Williams' *Sine Nomine* (B144, M536, L174, P42, RC80) springs immediately to mind. Hum through this tune for "For all the saints" and note each of the three elements mentioned above.

One test of an adequate hymn melody is its impressiveness when sung unadorned by harmony. Unison singing is considered such a desideratum by some denominations that the pew edition is a melody-only edition (see the Episcopal *Hymnal 1940*). Editors of hymnals with full music score will indicate at the beginning those tunes which should be sung in unison. Here are a few examples: *Slane* "Be thou my vision," (B212, M256, P303, RC169) *Purpose* "God is working his purpose out," (B509, P500, RC99) and *Lasst Uns Erfreuen* "All creatures of our God and King." (B9, M60, L527, P100, RC8)

2. Harmony

The harmony is the tonal garb of the melody. The character of the melody is modified, sometimes completely altered, by the type of harmonization. In the three unison tunes listed above, the harmonies are thickened or thinned according to the needs of the moment.

The enormous majority of hymn tunes have harmony in four parts. Although the soprano melody is the principal and iden-

23. From *Music in Worship: Report of the Archbishops' Committee,* appointed May 1922 (London: Central Board of Finance and S.P.C.K.)

tifying tune, ideally all other lines should have musical worth and individuality. In other words, a bass, tenor, or alto should find his or her vocal line as satisfying and challenging as the soprano line is to the soprano singers. Fortunately our hymnals are supplied with an increasing number of well-harmonized melodies. The J. S. Bach harmonizations of the German chorales are classic examples. Here are several additional illustrations: *Aberystwyth*, (B20, M125, L91, P216, RC293) *Arfon*, (M112, P197) *St. Columba*, (L456, P106, RC268) and *Darwall's 148th*. (B120, M483, L261, P14, RC235) Malcolm Williamson's *Mercer Street* (E108) (see page 78) contains many delightful surprises: the unexpectedness of the fourth chord, the forward thrust of the harmonies under the dotted whole notes, and the movement from the C natural to C sharp in the last two measures.

The harmonic palette of the musical artist is almost limitless. Notice the dynamic thrust given to the second and fourth lines of the stirring Irish traditional melody *Durrow* (P93)[24] by the dissonant second chord:

Another simple example of harmonic variation can be given. J. B. Dykes in his familiar tune *Nicaea* could have boringly harmonized the first phrase of "Holy, Holy, Holy! Lord God Almighty" (B1, M26, L165, P11, RC118) using only the tonic and subdominant chords:

As it is, Dykes used many different chords in this brief phrase:

24. Harmonized by David Evans. Used by permission of The Educational Company of Ireland Limited, Walkinstown, Dublin 12.

3. Rhythm (Time Measurement)

In its broadest sense, the word *rhythm* can identify all aspects of musical performance which contribute to a feeling of onward motion. The Greek verb *Rhein,* from which the word rhythm derives, means "to flow." A symphony, then, superbly played, takes us on a musical journey which unfolds beauties, surprises, excitements, tensions, resolutions.

The behavior of a hymn melody is influenced to a large extent by the variations of the lengths of its component tones. Fundamental to the notation of a hymn tune is the assumption that there will be an underlying predictable regular beat, just as all architecture assumes the constancy of length of an inch or a meter. Enough tones will occur on beats to give a unifying pulsation and enable the congregation to move forward together. But in most hymn melodies, there is a variety of note lengths which give rhythmic interest and propulsion to the singing.

There are some hymn melodies in which every note falls squarely on a beat. The "ironed out" version of *Old Hundredth* "Praise God from whom all blessings flow," (B6, P544) is an obvious example. Another is *Winchester New.* (M102, P242, RC218)

There are also many tunes whose mensuration is limited to two note values—a quarter and a half note such as *Eventide,* "Abide with me." (B217, M289, L272, P64) The 125 Genevan psalter tunes use mainly variations of these two time lengths. The original version of *Old Hundredth* employs two lengths, one twice as long as the other. The *Lutheran Book of Worship* (no.

245) authentically omits bar lines for this melody and indicates phrase endings by a little vertical mark as was done in the 1542 *La Forme des Prieres,* the first Genevan psalter. Here is the score. In the original, the last phrase began with three half notes.

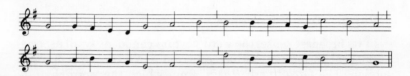

Old 124th, "Turn back, O Man" (M475, P490) and *Donne Secours,* "Hope of the world, thou Christ of great compassion" (L493, P285) are further examples of Genevan psalter tunes based on these two time values.

But many of these psalter tunes are enlivened by syncopations or tones which happen off the beat. A relatively familiar one is the tune *Psalm 42 (Freu Dich Sehr)* (B77, L29, RC60) which accompanies the Advent hymn "Comfort, comfort you my people." Here is its first line with check marks indicating the regular beats and showing how some notes occur off beat:

Another example of a psalter tune with syncopation is *Les Commandmens de Dieu (Commandments),* (M307, P59, RC263), "The day thou gavest, Lord, is ended."

Some recent hymnal editors continue to insert bar lines in these reformation melodies and thus confuse many organists and pianists. Here is an instance of this kind of barring of *Psalm 42* which might lead an instrumentalist to try to count measures of 3/4, 6/4, and 4/4 lengths. By concentrating on the quarter note value as the basic unit, the accompanist loses the stride of the half note which alone permits the syncopation to happen in the music:

Es Ist Ein Ros, "Lo, how a rose," (L58, P162, RC164) the original rhythmic version of *Ein Feste Burg*, "A mighty Fortress is our God," (L228, RC3) and *Gaudeamus Pariter*, "Come, you faithful, raise the strain" (L132, RC58) each have syncopation and need the pulsation of the half note.

It is significant that two leading denominational hymnals do not have time signatures (Episcopal 1940 and Lutheran 1978). The instrumentalists and singers must decide what note value is the basis for the beat.

4. Structure

Even within its brief compass, a well structured hymn tune will manifest the unity and variety of true art. Each of its phrases will be shaped so that the tones lead inevitably to the climax of the phrase, which frequently is the highest and/or longest note. And, just as important, the phrases must be so masterfully juxtaposed that the singers are led through lesser curves of energy to the central apex of the composition and then finally to the satisfaction of the final tone. An analysis of the tune *Lyons*, "O worship the King" (B30, M473, P26) is a rewarding study in tune architecture.

Within the structure of a popular hymn tune we find a variety of thematic repetitions. In the most familiar of Christmas carols, "Silent Night," (B89, M393, L65, P154, RC244) the first four-note theme is repeated four times. Some other examples of thematic patterns are:

AABA	*Ebenezer*, "Once to every man and nation" (B385, M242, P361, RC280)
	Forest Green, "All beautiful the march of days" (M33, P96)
ABB	*Morning Song*, "O Holy City, seen of John" (M481, P508, RC204)
AABBCCBBBBB	*Lasst Uns Erfreuen*, "All creatures of our God and King" (B9, M60, L527, P100, RC8)
ABBA	*Cormac*, "For the might of thine arm we bless thee" (M534)
ABCD	*Slane*, "Be thou my vision" (B212, M256, P303, RC169)

D. The Matching of Text and Tune

Words and music combine to convey the spiritual import of the hymn to the mind and heart of the Christian. Like a successful marriage of man and woman, the finest hymns are those which have a magnificent text and a strong, beautiful tune. Martin Luther and George Neumark each gave to Christianity a hymn which exemplifies fully this successful combining of words and music. Each composed both the text and the tune. The hymns are "A mighty Fortress is our God" (B37, M20, L228, P91, RC3) and "If thou but suffer God to guide thee." (B203, M210, L453, P344)

There are numerous instances where a strong hymn text has survived even though wedded for years to a weaker tune. Usually, but not always, these can be spotted in a hymnal by the presence of an alternate tune. As a rule the better tune—in the opinion of the editors—is given first, with the familiar but less desirable melody given second. This is done in the hope that congregations can gradually be weaned to the preferred tune. This was done in the case of the text "For all the saints." A number of hymnals a generation ago began adding Vaughan Williams' *Sine Nomine* (B144, M536, L174, P425, RC80) alongside the weaker tune *Sarum.* (M537, P425) The new setting has caught on so completely that recent hymnals have dropped *Sarum* altogether.

It is generally known among hymnologists that Dr. Fosdick desired that his hymn "God of grace and God of glory" (B265, M470, L415, P358) be sung to the tune *Regent Square* but now it is generally wedded to the Welsh melody *Cwm Rhondda.* Fosdick's opinion about this divorce and remarriage is interesting. In reply to an inquiry about this shift of tunes, he replied: "My secretary has already written you the answer to your question about my hymn's divorce from *Regent Square* and re-marriage to *Cwm Rhondda.* The Methodists did it! And both here and abroad they are being followed."[25]

The reader will note in the next chapter that the Consultation on Ecumenical Hymnody could not agree on a preferred tune to

25. Quoted in *Guide to the Pilgrim Hymnal* by Ronander and Porter. p. 287.

certain texts but proposed several and in one case ("O how shall I receive thee") they were undecided!

The tune *Terra Beata* for "This is my Father's world" (B155, M45, L554, P101) is being challenged by two other tunes. One excellent alternate is the tune *Mercer Street* by Malcolm Williamson, quoted on page 78. The other is *Kentucky 93rd,* (L246) recommended in the next chapter by the Consultation on Ecumenical Hymnody and printed as the first tune with this text in *The Hymnal of the United Church of Christ,* No. 33.

The two major considerations in determining compatibility of text and tune are metrical and emotional identity.

1. Identity of Meter

It goes without saying that the metrical patterns of text and music such as Short Meter and 76.76.D must be the same. In this connection, we should mention that ideally the accents of the words from stanza to stanza should fall in the same place. As an illustration, observe how Henry van Dyke in "Joyful, joyful, we adore Thee" (B31, M38, L551, P21, RC154) was able to align the accented syllables. This means that the primary and secondary accents of each 4/4/ measure in the tune *Hymn To Joy* (the first and third beats) coincide with the accented syllables of the words, thus emphasizing the speech rhythm:

1.	Joy -	ful	joy -	ful,	we	a -	dore	Thee,
2.	All	Thy	works	with	joy	sur -	round	Thee,
3.	Thou	art	giv -	ing	and	for -	giv -	ing,
4.	Mor -	tals,	join	the	hap -	py	cho -	rus.

Most of the Watts and Wesley hymns also exhibit this consistency of accents from stanza to stanza.

Contrast this with the beginning of the third phrases of the eight stanzas in "For all the saints." (B144, M536, L174, P425, RC80)

1.	Thy	name,	O	Je -	sus,	be	for -	ev -	er	blest,
2.		Thou,	in the	dark -	ness	drear,	their	one	true	Light,
3.	And	win	with	them	the	vic -	tor's	crown	of	gold,
4.	Yet	all	are	one	in	Thee,	for	all	are	Thine,
5.	And	hearts	are	brave	a -	gain,	and	arms	are	strong,

6.		Sweet	is the	calm	of	par	- a -	dise	the	blest,
7.	The	King	of	glo -	ry	pass	- es	on	His	way,
8.		Sing -	ing to	Fa -	ther,	Son,	and	Ho -	ly	Ghost.

This disparity of stanza accents (found to a degree in most hymns but exceptionally illustrated in this particular one) can either be forced into the stiff accentual pattern of a hymn tune (*Sarum*) or else an especially elastic tune can be shaped to fit the shifting stresses, as is shown in the magnificent tune *Sine Nomine*. For other illustrations of solutions to this problem, study these two tunes: Martin Shaw's tune *Purpose* for "God is working his purpose out" (B509, P500, RC99) and *New Dance* by Richard Wetzel for Auden's "He is the Way." (E72)

Having observed congregations stumble at these points of disparity or neglect to slip in two syllables where the preceding stanza had only one, the writer is inclined to agree with Robert Bridges, former poet laureate of England, who was discussing with a friend "whether the accented notes in the tune required always a corresponding accent in the words." He wrote:

> I think that the intelligent hymn-singer is getting much too squeamish on this head. I do not find that an occasional disagreement between accent of words and music offends me in a hymn. A fine tune is an unalterable artistic form, which pleases in itself and for itself. The notion of its giving way to the words is impossible. The words are better suited if they fit with *all* the quantities and accents of the tune, but it is almost impossible and not necessary that they should. Their *mood* is what the tune must be true to; and the mood is the main thing. If the tune also incidentally reinforces important words or phrases, that is all the better, and where there are refrains, or repetitions of words, the tune should be designed for them; but the enormous power that the tune has of enforcing or even of creating a mood is the one invaluable thing of magnitude, which overrules every other consideration.[26]

Comprehension of the text is also furthered by the completion of a unit of thought within a single phrase or clause. Thus the musical and textual units coincide. To be specific, the congregation should not too often have to take a breath between the verb and its direct object. Here again we find models of conciseness in this matter with hymns of Wesley and Watts. Indeed, Watts in

---

26. From a letter written by Robert Bridges in 1911, published in the Church Music Society Occasional Paper 11 (Oxford University Press).

his Preface to the Hymns (1707) is explicit about his intentions in this regard: "I have seldom permitted a stop in the middle of a line, and seldom left the end of a line without one, to comport a little with the unhappy mixture of reading and singing which cannot presently be reformed."

2. Identity of Emotion

As Robert Bridges stated above, there is an emotional tone to both text and tune and these should be mutually reinforcing. A poem extolling the greatness of our God and His creation must have music of nobility and loftiness. In the words of Dr. Benson:

> The hymn and its tune together compose the unit of the hymn as sung, and together stand or fall. An inartistic tune will kill the most poetic hymn ever written. A dull or unwelcome tune will impart to the most spiritual words an atmosphere of insincerity that makes one's spirit shrink, A tune adequate to the spiritual values of the words interprets them. A great tune does more; it adds something to the printed words by way of suggesting things of the spirit unprinted between the lines.[27]

27. From Louis F. Benson, *The Hymnody of the Christian Church.* p. 232. Richmond: John Knox Press, 1956.

Chapter V

A CHRONOLOGICAL ECUMENICAL LIST OF BASIC HYMNS

What are the most important hymns in a denominational hymnal? Is there a nucleus with which an enterprising church leader can begin? We have been citing text and tune examples from five denominational hymnals. Here are the number of hymns in each of them:

	hymn total
Roman Catholic *Worship II* 1975	313
Baptist Hymnal 1975	512
Methodist *The Book of Hymns* 1964, 1966	552
Lutheran Book of Worship 1978	569
Presbyterian *The Hymnbook* 1955	527

Since we can hardly expect the ordinary congregation to sing a majority of the contents of a denominational hymnal, we need a list of basic hymns which are sung by Christians of many denominations. This chapter provides such a list and it was compiled by a group of hymn enthusiasts representing a number of leading denominations of North America.

When the United Church of Christ formed a hymnal committee in 1966, its General Synod instructed the group to produce a hymnal consonant with the ecumenical spirit of the United Church. The Preface to their hymnal states "Early in the work a Consultation on Ecumenical Hymnody was called, bringing together representatives from most of the major communions to explore the possibilities of cooperation in the area of hymnody."[1] Churches represented in the Consultation were Disciples of

---

1. *The Hymnal of the United Church of Christ*, p. 6. Philadelphia: United Church Press, 1974.

Christ, Protestant Episcopal Church, Evangelical Covenant Church of North America, Lutheran Church (Missouri Synod, American Lutheran Church, and Lutheran Church of America), United Methodist Church, Moravian Church, United Presbyterian Church in the U.S.A., Presbyterian Church in the United States, Roman Catholic Church, United Church of Christ, and United Church of Canada.

This Consultation began its work in 1968.[2] The members did not expect to produce a single ecumenical hymnal but they did pay close attention to each other in the ensuing process of consultation. Their dialogue grew out of an expressed desire for a study of all hymnals in use by major Christian denominations on this continent to determine which hymns are common to our heritage, which hymns should by common consent be retained and which should be "retired," which tune should be used with each text, what is the best translation, and in some instances which stanzas should be used.

Following a review of six major hymnals by the Consultation members, a broader and more detailed study was undertaken by the Inter-Lutheran Commission on Worship. Recommendations concerning each hymn were made by the hymn text and hymn tune committees of this Commission. These recommendations were then presented to the members of the Consultation on Ecumenical Hymnody and, after balloting, 150 hymns were adopted in September, 1971. Because several significant hymnals were published following the completion of the original list, it was felt that additional materials should be considered. After several years of study, 77 more hymns were approved in September 1976 and they were integrated into a list of 227 hymns.

This list gives church leaders an idea of many of the basic hymns sung by millions of English-speaking Christians each Sunday. It should not be inferred that these are the 227 "best" hymns in existence, but we can conclude that these are hymns of high quality and are worthy of inclusion in the repertory of local congregations. This Consultation included many who were top experts in the field of hymnody,[3] and this list represents their

2. The work of this Consultation was described in an article "The Consultation on Ecumenical Hymnody" by Ford Battles and Morgan Simmons in *The Hymn*, April, 1977.
3. Reactions to this choice of ecumenical hymns were given in the April, 1978 issue of *The Hymn* in an article entitled "The CEH List: Four Diverse Appraisals" by Robert J. Batastini, Donald P. Hustad, Austin C. Lovelace, and Cyril V. Taylor.

considered judgment, reached after much study and conference. It is a more valuable hymnic resource than a statistical compilation reached by counting the occurences of certain hymns in major hymnals to determine the frequency of inclusion.

No single hymnal will have each of the following hymns but most of the major hymnals will include a considerable proportion of them. At least two hymnbooks (*The Hymnal of the United Church of Christ* 1974 and the *Lutheran Book of Worship* 1978 have an asterisk by each hymn title in its Index of First Lines to indicate those hymns which are included in the following ecumenical list.

It should be noted that the seven hymnals cited as sources in this chapter do not always have the exact title or translation recommended by the Consultation. The tunes for particular hymn texts differ in some of these hymnals from the Consultation's recommendation.

Since the following list is based on the *texts* of the 227 ecumenical hymns, there is appended to this chapter a brief outline of the major types of hymn *tunes* with a few examples of each school or era, and also a brief discussion of recent hymnody not included in this Consultation's list.

This ecumenical list is presented here in groups of hymns more or less chronologically arranged. A brief descriptive paragraph or so summarizes each of the historical periods. In a book of this nature, the description must of necessity be cursory. Several histories of hymnody are listed in the bibliography at the end of this volume. The title of each hymn is followed by the author and date of composition or publication, if known. Then is added the tune name recommended by the Consultation.

The entire list was printed in *The Hymn,* October, 1977 and can be secured from the Hymn Society of America. This HSA listing includes the names of hymnals which were consulted and the location of the preferred text and tune. It should be stated that this list is not officially endorsed by the Hymn Society of America but was published as useful information.

1. The Church's First Heritage of Song: The Psalms and Canticles of the Old Testament

The ancient Hebrews made extensive use of singing and of musical instruments. Many of the texts which expressed their praise and supplication came from the Book of Psalms. It will be recalled that Jesus and his disciples concluded the Last Supper by singing the Hallel Psalms 115-118.

Christians through the centuries have continued to sing and chant the psalms. In their *prose* form they have been set to Gregorian and Anglican chants. The *Lutheran Book of Worship* 1978 has included the entire psalter pointed for chanting. It also provides ten simple tones to which the psalms can be sung and a page of instructions (p. 290). Father Joseph Gelineau and other contemporary composers have put the prose psalms to congregational music. Examples of Gelineau psalms can be found in *Worship II* 1975 (21 entries) and *Ecumenical Praise* 1977 (2 entries).

In their *metrical* form the psalms have reached into almost every congregation. What church has not sung the Scottish version of the 23rd psalm "The Lord's my Shepherd, I'll not want?" The widespread use of metrical psalms was inaugurated by John Calvin's decision in Geneva to provide the 150 psalms translated into metrical French. Many of Calvin's followers on the continent and in England and Scotland adopted the custom of psalm singing. When Isaac Watts in 1719 issued the *Psalms of David Imitated,* he gave a new impetus to psalm usage in worship.

Examples of metrical psalms and psalm paraphrases are given in a number of the following sections of this chapter, especially in sections 6 and 8.

In addition to versions of the psalms, congregations have also sung what are called the Lesser Canticles of the Old Testament. They include the following: *Audite coeli* (Deut. 32:1-4, 9, 36, 40, 43); *Benedicite, omnia opera* (apocryphal Song of the Three Young Men, added in the Septuagint to the Hebrew Daniel); *Cantemus Domino* (Ex. 15:1-2, 6, 11, 13, 17-18); *Confitebor tibi* (Is. 12); *Domine, audivi* (Hab. 3:2-6, 13, 18-19); *Exultavit cor meum* (I Sam. 2:1-10); *Song of David* (I Chron. 29:10-18); and *Song of Hezekiah* (Is. 38:10-20).

2. Hymns and Canticles of the New Testament

Early fragmentary references lead us to believe that the vitality of the new Christian faith expressed itself in an outburst of song. Christ's birth was heralded by the heavenly hosts singing "Glory to God in highest heaven, And on earth his peace for men on whom his favour rests." (NEB, Luke 2:14) We have already mentioned that our Lord hallowed for all time the use of music by joining his disciples in singing before they went out into the garden of Gethsemane. Paul urged the Ephesians and Colossians to teach and admonish one another with psalms and hymns and spiritual songs (Ephesians 5:18-20; Colossians 3:17-27). The second chapter of his letter to the Philippians is believed by many scholars to be a hymn.

The Greater Canticles, found in the New Testament, include the *Benedictus* (Luke 1:68-79); the *Magnificat* (Luke 1:46-55); and the *Nunc Dimittis* (Luke 2:29-32). The *Te Deum Laudamus*, though not from the Bible, is also considered one of the major canticles. These canticles have been included in many of the principal liturgies of Christendom.

The Angelic Song *Gloria in Excelsis* (Luke 2:14) in expanded form is a part of the liturgy of many churches, especially concluding the Communion Service. It is usually either chanted with a Scottish melody or is sung in the metrical version "All glory be to God on high." (L166)

3. Greek Hymnody

During the first few centuries of the Christian era, Greek-speaking converts around the eastern Mediterranean penned some immortal hymns. These texts, frequently rising from bitter persecution and fierce doctrinal struggles, are loved and sung even to this day.

Come, ye faithful, raise the strain (M448, L132, P205, RC58) John of Damascus, 675-749?	*Gaudeamus Pariter/Ave Virgo Virginum*
Father, we thank Thee who hast planted (M307, E1, RC79) the *Didache,* c. 110	*Rendez À Dieu*
Let all mortal flesh keep silence (M324, L198, P148, RC157) c. fifth century	*Picardy*
Lord Jesus, think on me (M284, L309, P270, RC167) Synesius, c. 375-430	*Southwell*
O gladsome light, O grace (L279, P61, RC197) c. third century	*Nunc Dimittis*
The King shall come when morning dawns (M353, L33, P232, RC269)	*Consolation* (from *Kentucky Harmony*)

4. Latin Hymnody

One of the largest reservoirs of modern Christian song is Latin hymnody. The era from which most of this treasure came stretched for a millennium from about 400-1400 A.D.—the so-called Middle Ages. It began principally with Ambrose, Bishop of Milan, (340-397) and Prudentius (348-c.413) and reached almost to the birth of the Protestant Reformation. These hymns were written by men from various strata of the Latin Church, ranging from Pope Gregory I (540-604) to an abbot (Bernard of Clairvaux, 1091-1153) and a bishop (Theodulph of Orleans, c. 760-c. 821) down to a monk in a stone cell, Bernard of Cluny in the 12th century. Beyond the walls of the monastery we find the wandering friar, Francis of Assisi (1182-1226).

Most of these hymns were written for one of the many daily monastic services of worship called Offices which were celebrated every three hours in the chapel. The hymn "Creator of the stars of night" was sung at vespers during Advent. A major translator of this corpus was John Mason Neale (1818-1866) whose skill as a linguist and poet is attested by the number of his translations of Latin and Greek hymns in our present-day hymnals. The recent Methodist hymnal (1964, 1966) included fifteen of Neale's translations.

All creatures of our God and King   *Lasst Uns Erfreuen*
  (B9, M60, L527, P100, RC8)
  Francis of Assisi, c. 1225
All glory, laud, and honor   *St. Theodulph*
  (B39, M424, L108, P187, RC9)
  Theodulph of Orleans, c. 820
Christ, thou art the sure foundation   *Regent Square*
  (M298, L367, P433, E20, C52, RC43)
  Anon. c. 7th century
Come down, O love divine   *Down Ampney*
  (M466, L508, RC49)
  Bianco da Siena, c. 1367
Creator of the stars of night   *Conditor Alma*
  (M78, RC65)
  Anon. 9th century
Father, we praise thee, now the night is over   *Christe Sanctorum*
  (M504, L267, P43, RC78)
  Pope Gregory the Great, 540-604
Hail thee, festival day   *Salve, Feste Dies*
  (L142, RC109)
  Fortunatus, 530-609

Hark, a thrilling voice is sounding (L37) Anon. 1632	*Merton*
Jesus Christ is risen today (B115, M443, L151, P204, RC145) Anon. 14th century	*Easter Hymn*
Jesus, the very thought of thee (B73, M82, L316, P401) Anon. 11th century	*St. Paul's Kingston*
Jesus, thou joy of loving hearts (B72, M329, L356, P215, RC149) Anon. c. 12th century	*Song 5*
My God, I love thee not because (B57, L491) Spanish, 17th century	*Kingsfold*
O come, O come, Emmanuel (B78, M354, L34, P147, RC195) Anon. 12th century	*Veni Emmanuel*
O Holy Spirit, by whose breath (RC205) Anon. 9th century	*Veni Creator* *Komm, Gott Schöpfer*
O love, how deep, how broad, how high (L88, E26) Anon. 15th century	*Deo Gracias*
O sons and daughters (M451, L139, P206, RC312) Tisserand, d. 1494	*O Filii Et Filiae*
O splendor of God's glory bright (M29, L271, P46) Ambrose, 340–397	*Puer Nobis*
Of the Father's love begotten (B62, M357, L42, P7, RC216) Prudentius, 348–c.413	*Divinum Mysterium*
On Jordan's banks the Baptist's cry (L36, RC218) Coffin, 1736	*Winchester New*
The strife is o'er, the battle done (M447, L135, P203, RC273) Anon. 17th century	*Victory*
What star is this (RC305) Coffin, 1736	*Puer Nobis*
Where charity and love prevail (B257, L126, RC287) Anon. c. 9th century	*Christian Love*

5. German and Scandinavian Hymnody

The hymnody of northern Europe centered around the Reformation begun by Martin Luther (1483-1546) but its precursors were the abundant folk hymns of the preceding centuries and the songs of such groups as the Bohemian Brethren whose earliest recorded hymnal work was dated 1505. Their leader was John Hus (1369-1415). Luther's intent regarding music, and especially congregational singing, is seen in this letter which he wrote in 1523 to his friend the court chaplain, George Spalatin: "Following the example of the prophets and fathers of the church, I intend to make German Psalms for the people, i.e., spiritual songs so that the Word of God even by means of song may live among the people."[4]

Luther's teaching and example influenced countless poets to express their faith through hymns. This occurred especially during the Thirty Years War (1618-1648).

A mighty fortress is our God (B37, M20, L228, P91, E25, RC3) Martin Luther, 1529	*Ein' Feste Burg*
Ah, holy Jesus, how hast thou offended (M412, L123, P191, RC6) Heermann, 1630	*Herzliebster Jesu*
All glory be to God on high (L166) Decius, 1539	*Allein Gott in Der Höh*
All my heart this night rejoices (M379, L46, P172, RC12) Gerhardt, 1653	*Warum Sollt Ich*
Blessed Jesus, at thy word (M257, L248, RC37) Clausnitzer, 1663	*Liebster Jesu*
Break forth, O beauteous heavenly light (M373) Rist, 1641	*Schop*
Built on a rock the church doth stand (B235, L365, P432) Grundtvig, 1837 Danish	*Kirken Den Er Et*
Children of the heavenly Father (B207, M521, L474) Berg, 1858. Swedish.	*Tryggare Kan Ingen Vara*
Christ is arisen (L136) Weisse, 1531	*Christ Ist Erstanden*
Christ Jesus lay in death's strong bonds (M438, L134, RC45) Luther, 1524	*Christ Lag*
Comfort, comfort ye my people (B77, L29, RC60) Olearius, 1671	*Psalm 42*

4. From *Liturgy and Hymns,* edited by Ulrich S. Leupold, p. 221, in Luther's Works, Vol. 53. Philadelphia: Fortress Press. 1965.

Deck thyself with joy and gladness (M318, L224) Franck, 1649	*Schmücke Dich*
Fairest Lord Jesus (B48, M79, L518, P135) Anon. pub. 1677	*Schönster Herr Jesu*
From heaven above to earth I come (L51, P173, RC89) Luther, 1535	*Vom Himmel Hoch*
Give to the winds thy fears (B224, M51, P364) Gerhardt, 1653	*St. Bride*
Good Christian men, rejoice (B123, M391, L55, P165, RC105) Anon. German/Latin, 14th century	*In Dulci Jubilo*
Holy God, we praise thy name (M8, L535, RC117) Anon. c. 1774	*Te Deum/Grosser Gott*
If thou but suffer God to guide thee (B203, M210, L453, P344) Neumark, c. 1640	*Neumark*
Jesus, priceless treasure (M220, L457, P414) Franck, 1653	*Lindeman*
Jesus, still lead on (B500, L341, P334) Zinzendorf, 1721	*Seelenbräutigam*
Jesus, thy boundless love (B326, M259, L336, P404) Gerhardt, 1653	*David's Harp*
Let all together praise our God (M389, L47, RC160) Hermann, 1560	*Lobt Gott, Ihr Christen*
Lift up your heads, ye mighty gates (M363, L32, P152, RC163) Weissel, 1642	*Truro*
Lo, how a rose e'er blooming (L58, P162, RC164) Anon. pub. 1599	*Es Ist Ein' Ros'*
Lord Jesus Christ, be present (L253) Attributed to Wilhelm II, Duke of Saxe-Weimar, 1598-1662)	*Herr Jesu Christ, Dich Zu Uns Wend*
Now thank we all our God (B234, M49, L533, P9, RC189) Rinkart, 1636	*Nun Danket Alle Gott*
O God, thou faithful God (L504) Heermann, 1630	*Darmstadt*
O how shall I receive thee (L23) Gerhardt, 1653	Tune: Undecided

O Morning Star, how fair and bright (M399, L76, P415) Nicolai, 1599	*Wie Schön Leuchtet*
O sacred Head, now wounded (B105, M418, L116, P194, RC211) Latin translated by Gerhardt, 1656	*Passion Chorale*
Open now thy gates of beauty (M13, L250, P40, RC222) Schmolck, 1732	*Neander*
Out of the deep I cry (M526, L295, RC224) Luther, 1523	*Aus Tiefer Not Schrei*
Praise to the Lord, the Almighty (B10, M55, L543, P1, RC231) Neander, 1680	*Lobe Den Herren*
Rejoice, rejoice believers (L25, P231) Laurenti, 1700	*Vigil*
Silent Night (B89, M393, L65, P154, RC244) Mohr, 1818	*Stille Nacht*
Sing praise to God who reigns above (B22, M4, P15, RC249) Schütz, 1675	*Sei Lob Und Ehr*
Sleepers, wake! the watch are calling (M366, L31) Nicolai, 1597	*Wachet Auf*
The duteous day now closeth (L276, P66) Gerhardt, 1647	*Innsbruck*
We plough the fields and scatter (M513, L362, P524) Claudius, 1782	*Wir Pflügen*
What God has done is rightly done (L446, P366) Rodigast, 1676	*Was Gott Tut*
When morning gilds the skies (B44, M91, L545, P41) Anon. 19th century	*Laudes Domini*

6. Metrical Psalmody

The reformer John Calvin (1509-1564) knew the power of song to "inflame the hearts of men to invoke and praise God with a more vehement and ardent zeal."[5] He restricted his use of texts for his church songs mainly to the Psalms and his logic for doing this is as follows: "Although we look far and wide and search on

5. From *Source Readings in Music History* by Oliver Strunk, pp. 345-348. (Copyright © by W. W. Norton & Company, Inc. Used by permission.)

every hand, we shall not find better songs nor songs better
suited to that end than the Psalms of David which the Holy
Spirit made and uttered through him. And for this reason, when
we sing them we may be certain that God puts the words in our
mouths as if Himself sang in us to exalt His glory."[6]

The first Genevan psalter, though incomplete, appeared in
1542 in metrical French accompanied by melodies.[7] The com-
pleted psalter with all 150 psalms and 125 melodies was published in 1564. Already by that time metrical psalters in English
had been translated by Calvin's British followers. The first complete one (1562) was called "The Old Version" and was compiled
by Thomas Sternhold and John Hopkins. The Scottish version
was issued as part of *The Book of Common Order* in 1564. Thus
Calvin's followers on the continent and especially in England
and Scotland became psalm singers. About 60 years later the
Pilgrims brought the Ainsworth psalter[8] to the New World and
introduced metrical psalms into America. Twenty years after
landing at Plymouth, they published the first book in English-
speaking America, the *Bay Psalm Book*.

Let us with a gladsome mind (B27, M61, L521, P28) John Milton, 1623. Psalm 136	*Monkland*
The Lord's my Shepherd (B341, M68, L451, P104) *Scottish Psalter,* 1650. Psalm 23	*Crimond*
The Lord will come and not be slow (B128, M468, L318, P230) John Milton, 1648	*Old 107th*
Through all the changing scenes of life (M56) *The New Version,* 1696. Psalm 34	*Irish*

7. The Gathering Stream of British Hymnody

Although many British congregations from the time of the
Reformation (early to mid-16th century) until Isaac Watts (early
18th century) sang only metrical Old Testament psalms, there
were during this period hymn writers who wanted to express

6. Ibid.
7. Facsimile edition published and copyright © 1959 by Bärenreiter-Verlag Kassel.
   Edited by Pierre Pidoux.
8. See Waldo Selden Pratt, *The Music of the Pilgrims.* Boston: Oliver Ditson Co., 1921.
   Reprint edition: AMS Press, 1966.

their devotion in New Testament thought. So for many years in the British Isles these isolated streams of lyric expression had been gathering.

All praise to thee, my God this night (B43, M493, L278, P63, RC16) Ken, 1695	*Tallis' Canon*
Let all the world in every corner sing (B24, M10, P22, RC159) Herbert, 1633	*St. Teilo*
My song is love unknown (B486, L94, RC183) Crossman, 1664	*Love Unknown*
Praise God from whom all blessings flow (B7, L564, P544, E40, RC14) Ken, 1695	*Old Hundredth*
When all thy mercies, O my God (B468, M70, L264, P119) Addison, 1712	*Winchester Old*
While shepherds watched their flocks (B97, M394, P169, RC309) Tate, 1700	*Winchester Old*

8. Isaac Watts: His Psalms and Hymns

Isaac Watts (1674–1748), frequently called the "Father of English Hymnody," is generally credited with being mainly responsible for loosening the exclusive hold of metrical psalms in the English Church. His hymns such as "When I survey the wondrous cross" and his Christianized psalms such as "Jesus shall reign" (Psalm 72) speeded the emancipation. His essays on the need for renovation of psalmody also paved the way.

Before Jehovah's aweful throne (M22, L531, P81) 1706, 1719. Psalm 100	*Winchester New*
Come, let us join our cheerful songs (B126, L254, RC51) 1707	*Graefenberg/Nun Danket All'*
From all that dwell below the skies (M14, L550, P33, E40, RC86) 1719. Psalm 117	*Lasst Uns Erfreuen*
I sing the mighty power of God (M37, P84, RC133) 1715	*Ellacombe*
I'll praise my Maker while I've breath (M9) 1719. Psalm 146	*Old 113th*

Jesus shall reign	*Duke Street*
(B282, M472, L530, P496, RC147)	
1719. Psalm 72	
Joy to the world	*Antioch*
(B88, M392, L39, P161, E36, C18, RC153)	
1719. Psalm 98	
My Shepherd will supply my need	*Resignation*
(RC182)	
1719. Psalm 23	
Our God, our help in ages past	*St. Anne*
(B223, M28, L320, P111, RC203)	
1719. Psalm 90	
When I survey the wondrous cross	*Hamburg*
(B111, M435, L482, P198)	
1707	

9. The Hymns of the Wesleys

The Wesley brothers, John (1703–1791) and Charles (1707–1788), went the length and breadth of Britain preaching and singing the Gospel of Christ. In this Great Awakening, Charles was the hymn writer, composing over 6,500 hymns. John translated some fine German texts (see "Give to the winds thy fears"). Together they edited many hymnals. Both men were keenly aware of the need for an educational approach to evangelistic music as described in Chapter 2 with John's Directions for Singing.

A charge to keep I have	*Boylston*
(B407, M150, P301)	
C. Wesley, 1762	
Christ the Lord is risen today	*Llanfair*
(B114, M439, L130, RC46)	
C. Wesley, 1739	
Christ whose glory fills the sky	*Ratisbon*
(M401, L265, P47, E34)	
C. Wesley, 1740	
Come, thou long-expected Jesus	*Jefferson*
(B79, M360, L30, P151, RC57)	
C. Wesley, 1744	
Forth in thy name	*Song 34*
(M152, L505)	
C. Wesley, 1749	
Hail the day that sees him rise	*Llanfair*
(RC108)	
C. Wesley, 1739	
Hark! the herald angels sing	*Mendelssohn*
(B83, M388, L60, P163, RC111)	
C. Wesley, 1739	

Lo, he comes with clouds descending (M364, L27, P234) C. Wesley, 1758 and Cennick, 1750	*Helmsley*
Love divine, all loves excelling (B58, M283, L315, P399, RC172) C. Wesley, 1747	*Hyfrydol*
O for a thousand tongues to sing (B69, M1, L559, P141) C. Wesley, 1739	*Azmon*
Rejoice, the Lord is King (B120, M483, L171, P140, E32, RC235) C. Wesley, 1746	*Darwall's 148th*
Ye servants of God, your master proclaim (B292, M409, L252, P27, E33) C. Wesley, 1744	*Lyons*

10. Other Eighteenth-Century British Hymnody

In addition to the outstanding works of Watts and the Wesleys, the eighteenth century produced countless other hymn writers, notably two Calvinists, William Cowper (1731-1800) and John Newton (1725-1807), who in 1779 issued a collection called *Olney Hymns.* The winnowing process of the years has left us the following choice hymns:

All hail the power of Jesus' name (B40, M71, L328, P132, RC10) Perronet, 1779	*Coronation*
Amazing grace (B165, M92, L448, P275, RC22) Newton, 1779	*Amazing grace*
Come, thou almighty King (B2, M3, L522, P244, RC55) Anon. 1757.	*Italian Hymn/Moscow*
Come, thou fount of every blessing (B13, M93, L499, P379) Robinson, 1758	*Nettleton*
Glorious things of thee are spoken (M293, L358, P434, RC92) Newton, 1779	*Austria*
God moves in a mysterious way (B439, M215, L483, P112, E41) Cowper, 1774	*Dundee*
Great God, we sing that mighty hand (M509, P527) Doddridge, 1755	*Wareham*
Guide me, O thou great Jehovah (B202, M271, L343, P339) Williams, 1745	*Cwm Rhondda*

Hail, thou once despised Jesus (M454, P210) Attributed to Bakewell, pub. 1757	*Conquerer/O Durchbrecher*
Hark the glad sound, the Savior comes (L35) Doddridge, 1735	*Richmond*
How firm a foundation (B383, M48, L507, P369, RC121) Anon. 1787	*Foundation*
How sweet the name of Jesus sounds (B464, M81, L345, P130, RC125) Newton, 1779	*St. Peter*
Lord, dismiss us with thy blessing (M165, L259, P79) Fawcett, 1773	*Sicilian Mariners*
O come, all ye faithful (B81, M386, L45, P170, RC193) Wade, c. 1743	*Adeste Fideles*
O God of Bethel, by whose hand (L477, P342) Doddridge, 1736	*Dundee*
Praise the Lord, ye heavens adore him (B11, M42, P3, RC229) Anon. 1796	*Austria*
Praise to God, immortal praise Barbauld, 1772.	*Song 13*

11. Early Nineteenth-Century British Hymnody

In the early nineteenth century the literary world witnessed a renascence of wonder which expressed itself in interest in the world of nature (the poems of Wordsworth). It included also a romantic review of ancient culture and history (the novels of Walter Scott.) In hymnody Bishop Reginald Heber (1783–1826) influenced congregational song by producing enduring texts with depth of religious feeling and beauty of expression.

There was also a considerable effort to revitalize the Church of England during these early decades. A movement centering in Oxford, England had its start with a memorable sermon on "National Apostasy," preached by the brilliant John Keble in the early 1830s. This Oxford Movement produced not only the following original hymns but also led to the translation of many ancient Latin and Greek hymns listed above in Sections 3 and 4.

Blest are the pure in heart (M276, P226) Keble, 1819	*Franconia*

Bread of the world in mercy broken (M320, P445) Heber, 1827	*Rendez À Dieu*
Brightest and best of the sons of the morning (M400, L84, P175) Heber, 1811	*Stella Orientis*
Faith of our fathers, living still (B143, M151, L500, P348, RC75) Faber, 1849	*St. Catherine*
Holy, Holy, Holy, Lord Gold Almighty (B1, M26, L165, P11, RC118) Heber, 1826	*Nicaea*
New every morning is the love (M499, P45) Keble, 1822	*Melcombe*
Ride on, ride on in majesty (M425, L121, P188) Milman, pub. 1827	*The King's Majesty*
Sun of my soul, thou Savior dear (M502, P56) Keble, 1820	*Hursley*
There's a wideness in God's mercy (B171, M69, L290, P110, RC275) Faber, 1854	*Gott Will's Machen*

12. Nineteenth-Century British Hymnody: General

Technical histories of hymnody arrange the vast hymnic output of nineteenth-century Britain in such categories as (1) the Broad Church School, (2) the Evangelical School, and (3) the Anglican High Church School. To trace such currents is beyond the scope of this listing. However, it should be remarked that we owe a debt of gratitude to Britain for the following hymns of worth.

Abide with me (B217, M289, L272, P64) Lyte, 1847	*Eventide*
Alleluia, sing to Jesus (L158, RC19) Dix, 1866	*Hyfrydol*
Angels from the realms of glory (B87, M382, L50, P168, RC23) Montgomery, 1816	*Regent Square*
As with gladness men of old (M397, L82, P174, RC27) Dix, 1858	*Dix*
At even, when the sun was set (M501, P55) Twells, 1868	*Angelus*

At the name of Jesus   *King's Weston*
  (B363, M76, L179, P143, RC30)
  Noel, 1870
Come unto me, ye weary   *Meirionydd*
  (P268)
  Dix, pub. 1867
Come, ye thankful people, come   *St. George's Windsor*
  (B233, M522, L407, P525, RC59)
  Alford, 1844
Crown him with many crowns   *Diademata*
  (B52, M455, L170, P213, RC63)
  Bridges, 1851
Eternal Father, strong to save   *Melita*
  (M538, L467, P521, RC71)
  Whiting, 1860
Fight the good fight   *Grace Church, Gananoque*
  (B394, M241, L461, P359)
  Monsell, 1863
For all the saints   *Sine Nomine*
  (B144, M536, L174, P425, RC80)
  How, 1864
For the beauty of the earth   *Dix*
  (B54, M35, L561, P2, RC81)
  Pierpoint, 1864
Go to dark Gethsemane   *Gethsemane/Petra/*
  (B112, M434, L109, P193)   *Redhead 76/St. Prisca*
  Montgomery, 1825
God is my strong salvation   *Rex Summae Majestatis*
  (B343, M211, P347)
  Montgomery, 1822
God the omnipotent! King who ordainest   *Russian Hymn*
  (M544, L462, P487)
  Chorley, 1842 / Ellerton, 1870
Hail to the Lord's annointed   *Ellacombe*
  (M359, L87, P146, RC110)
  Montgomery, 1821
Here, O my Lord, I see thee face to face   *Farley Castle*
  (M326, L211, P442)
  Bonar, 1855
Immortal, invisible, God only wise   *St. Denio*
  (B32, M27, L526, P85, RC135)
  Smith, 1867
In heavenly love abiding   *Nyland*
  (B204, M230, P417, RC138)
  Waring, 1850
In the bleak midwinter   *Cranham*
  (M376)
  Rossetti, c. 1872
In the cross of Christ I glory   *Rathbun*
  (B70, M416, L104, P195)
  Bowring, 1825
Look, ye saints, the sight is glorious   *Bryn Calfaria*

(B121, M453, L156, P133)
Kelly, 1809

Make me a captive, Lord	*Corona*
(M184, P308)	
Matheson, 1890	
O God of love, O King of peace	*Wilderness*
(L414, P483, RC201)	
Baker, 1861	
O Lord of heaven and earth and sea	*Es Ist Kein Tag*
(M523)	
Wordsworth, 1863	
O perfect love, all human thought	*Perfect Love*
transcending	
(B395, M333, L287, P453)	
Gurney, 1883	
O spirit of the living God	*Melcombe*
(L388, P242)	
Montgomery, 1823	
O worship the King	*Hanover*
(B30, M473, L548, P26)	
Grant, 1833	
Once in royal David's city	*Irby*
(P462, RC220)	
Alexander, 1848	
Praise, my soul, the King of heaven	*Praise My Soul*
(B8, M66, L549, P31, RC228)	
Lyte, 1834	
Praise the Lord, his glories show	*Gwalchmai*
(P4)	
Lyte, 1834	
Savior, again to thy dear name we raise	*Ellers*
(B65, M236, L262, P77)	
Ellerton, 1866	
Shepherd of souls, refresh	*St. Flavian*
(RC242)	
Montgomery, 1825	
Sing to the Lord of harvest	*Wie Lieblich Ist Der Maien*
(B232, L412)	
Monsell, 1866	
Son of God, eternal Savior	*In Babilone*
(L364, RC254)	
Lowry, 1893	
Spirit divine, attend our prayers	*Grafenburg/Nun Danket All'*
(M461, P243, RC256)	
Reed, 1829	
Stand up and bless the Lord	*Festal Song*
(B26, M16)	
Montgomery, 1824	
Strong son of God, immortal love	*Song 34/Angel's Song*
(M146, P228)	*Astelpah*
Tennyson, 1850	
Take my life and let it be consecrated	*Patmos*

(B373, M187, L406, P310)
Havergal, 1873
The Church's one foundation   *Aurelia*
   (B236, M297, L369, P437, RC262)
Stone, 1866
The day thou gavest, Lord, is ended   *Commandments*
   (M500, L274, P59, RC263)
Ellerton, 1870
The head that once was crowned with thorns   *St. Magnus*
   (B125, M458, L173, P211, RC266)
Kelly, 1820
The King of love my shepherd is   *St. Columba*
   (B215, M67, L456, P106, RC268)
Baker, 1868
Thine arm, O Lord, in days of old   *St. Matthew*
   (L431, P179)
Plumptre, 1864
Thou whose almighty word   *Italian Hymn/Moscow*
   (B303, M480, L400)
Marriott, 1813
Watchman, tell us of the night   *Aberystwyth*
   (M358, P149, RC293)
Bowring, 1825
What child is this   *Greensleeves*
   (M385, L40, P159, RC303)
Dix, 1865

13. Twentieth-Century British Hymnody

The following ten hymns are excellent contributions from
Britain but unfortunately they do not include examples from the
pens of outstanding contemporary hymnists like Fred Kaan
(1929-), Brian Wren (1936-), and Fred Pratt Green (1903-).
The Consultation on Ecumenical Hymnody probably thought
that time was needed to determine which of their hymns had
long lasting value. At the conclusion of the Consultation's list, I
will mention some examples of their work.

Christ is the world's true light   *St. Joan*
   (B274, M408, P492)
Briggs, 1931
Come risen Lord and deign to be our guest   *Sursum Corda*
   (L209, E69)
Briggs, 1931
Father eternal, ruler of creation   *Langham*
   (M469, L413, P486, RC76)
Houseman, 1919

Good Christian men, rejoice and sing   *Gelobt Sei Gott*
  (B123, M449, L144)
  Alington, 1925
In Christ there is no east or west   *McKee*
  (B258, M192, L359, P479, E86)
  Oxenham, 1908
Judge eternal, throned in splendor   *Rhuddlan*
  (M546, L418, P517, RC155)
  Holland, 1902
O God of earth and altar   *Llangloffan*
  (M484, L428, P511)
  Chesterton, 1906
This joyful Eastertide   *Vruechten*
  (B124, L149)
  Woodward, 1902
Thou judge, by whom each empire fell   *Nun Freut Euch/Er Ist*
  Dearmer, pub. 1925   *Gewislich An Der Zeit*
Ye watchers and ye holy ones   *Lasst Uns Erfreuen*
  (M19, L175, P34, RC313)
  Riley, 1906

14. Nineteenth-Century American Hymnody

The first full century of this new nation's life witnessed the pioneer expansion to the West, the frightful civil war, the growth of our industrial might, and three decades of the mass evangelistic campaigns of Dwight L. Moody (1837–1899) which had a strong influence in furthering gospel songs. From the Church of this relatively young country came the following ten hymns.

All things are thine, no gift have we   *Herr Jesu Christ Dich Zu*
  (M347, P313)   *Uns Wend*
  Whittier, 1873
Away in a manger   *Cradle Song*
  (B80, M384, L67, P157, RC34)
  Murray, pub. 1885
Dear Lord and Father of mankind   *Herman*
  (B270, M235, L506, P416)
  Whittier, 1872
Eternal Ruler of the ceaseless round   *Song 1*
  (L373, RC73)
  Chadwick, 1864
God of our fathers, whose almighty hand   *National Hymn*
  (B149, M552, L567, P515, RC101)
  Roberts, 1876
I love thy kingdom, Lord   *St. Thomas*
  (B240, M294, L368, P435)
  Dwight, 1800

O little town of Bethlehem (B85, M381, L41, P171, RC207) Brooks, 1868	*St. Louis*
O Master, let me walk with thee (B369, M170, L492, P304) Gladden, 1879	*Maryton*
O my soul, bless God the Father (B34, M65) Metrical version of Psalm 103, pub. 1871	*Stuttgart*
Thou art the way, to thee alone (M75, L464, P221, RC278) Doane, 1824	*Dundee*

15. Twentieth-Century American Hymnody

The stirring of social conscience, concern for deeper worship, prayer for world friendship and peace, the preservation of natural resources and environment, yearning for the Kingdom of God—these are some of the emphases found in contemporary American hymnody.

All beautiful the march of days (M33, P96) Wile, 1911	*Forest Green*
Eternal God, whose power upholds (M476, P485, RC72) Tweedy, 1929	*Wellington Square*
Gentle Mary laid her child (M395, P167) Cook, 1919. Canadian	*Tempus Adest Floridum*
God of grace and God of glory (B265, M470, L415, P358, E116) Fosdick, 1930	*Restoration/Cwm Rhondda*
God of our life through all the circling years (M47, P108) Kerr, 1916	*Sandon*
God of the fertile fields Harkness, 1953	*Hinman*
Great is thy faithfulness (B216) Chisholm, 1923	*Faithfulness*
Hope of the world (B364, M161, L493, P291) Harkness, 1953	*Donne Secours/Geneva 12*
Joyful, joyful, we adore thee (B31, M38, L551, P21, RC154) Van Dyke, 1907	*Hymn to Joy*
Lord Christ, when first thou came'st (M355, L421, E88) Bowie, 1928	*Mit Freuden Zart*

Not alone for mighty empire   *Geneva*
  (M548, L437, P512)
  Merrill, 1909
O be joyful in the Lord   *Rock of Ages*
  Beach, 1958
O day of God, draw nigh   *St. Michael*
  (M477)
  Scott, 1937
O holy city, seen of John   *Sancta Civitas*
  (M481, P508, RC204)
  Bowie, 1909
Our Father, by whose name   *Rhosymedre*
  (L357, RC223)
  Tucker, 1939
Renew thy church   *All Is Well*
  Cober, 1960
This is my Father's world   *Kentucky 93rd*
  (B155, M45, L554, P101, E108, C57)
  Babcock, 1901
We praise thee, O God our Redeemer   *Kremser*
  (B15, L241, P17, RC296)
  Cory, 1902
Where cross the crowded ways of life   *Gardiner/Walton/Germany*
  (B311, M204, L429, P507)
  North, 1903

16. Miscellaneous Hymns: traditional, spiritual, folk.

Angels we have heard on high   *Gloria*
  (B95, M374, L71, P158, RC24)
  French traditional, first pub. 1855
Be thou my vision   *Slane*
  (B212, M256, P303)
  Anon. Irish, c. 8th century
Go, tell it on the mountain   *Go, Tell It*
  (B82, M404, L70, RC95)
  Negro spiritual
Infant holy, infant lowly   *W Zlobie Lezy*
  (B94, M396, L44, P164, RC141)
  Polish folk melody and text
Let us break bread together   *Let Us Break Bread*
  (B252, M330, L212, P447, RC162)
  American folk hymn
The first Nowell   *The First Nowell*
  (B91, M383, L56, P156)
  Traditional English
The God of Abraham praise   *Leoni/Yigdal*
  (B25, L544, P89, RC230)
  Traditional Jewish, c. 1400
Thine is the glory   *Judas Maccabeus*
  (M450, L145, P209, E107)
  Budry, 1884. Swiss

Were you there when they crucified my Lord   *Were You There*
  (B108, M436, L92, P201, RC302)
  Negro Spiritual
What wondrous love   *Wondrous Love*
  (B106, M432, L385, E46, RC306)
  American folk hymn

This concludes the list of 227 hymns selected by the Consultation on Ecumenical Hymnody. Following are several lists of texts and tunes prepared by the author to round out this survey of basic Christian hymns.

Gospel Songs

Gospel songs had their roots in the camp meetings which began in the early nineteenth century in Kentucky. Other influences which shaped this unique religious song form were the formation of the Salvation Army in England in the 1860s, the camp songs in the American Civil War, the founding of the Sunday School Movement with a long series of Sunday school songbooks of George Root, Bradbury, Lowry, and others. The evangelistic campaigns of Dwight L. Moody and Ira D. Sankey gave special impetus to the adoption of the genre. Here are a few examples of gospel songs which have enduring qualities:

Blessed assurance, Jesus is mine   Fanny J. Crosby
Take the name of Jesus with you   Lydia Baxter
I need Thee every hour   Annie S. Hawks
I love to tell the story   Katherine Hankey
What a friend we have in Jesus   Joseph Scriven
He leadeth me, O blessed thought   Joseph Gilmore
My hope is built on nothing less   Edward Mote

Hymnody 1956–1981

This quarter of a century witnessed an astounding amount of experimentation with church songs. There is no doubt that the emergence of pop music in almost every denomination had some of its roots in a musical explosion in east London in 1956. The London *Daily Express* reported "a screaming of jazz trumpets marked the Lord's Prayer during an Anglican Holy Communion Service, in which the traditional church music was replaced by boogie, beguine and calypso." The Rev. Geoffrey Beaumont had written and performed the *20th Century Folk Mass*. Furthermore, he and some friends formed "The 20th Century Church Light Music group" which published *Thirty 20th Century Hymn Tunes*. The Preface to this collection states that "They are offered in the belief that not only the great and lasting music of the past but also the ordinary and transient music of today—which is the background to the lives of so many—has a rightful place in our worship."[9]

This bold experimentation raised the eyebrows of many traditionalists but it opened the sluice gates and set tidal waves going throughout Christendom. In 1966 the Youth Departments of the World Council of Churches published *New Hymns for a New Day* including 44 songs. Among them were Sydney Carter's "Lord of the Dance," "Every star shall sing a carol," and "The devil wore a crucifix." Also included were "Oh freedom" and "We shall overcome."

In America, shortly after Beaumont's *Mass,* composers in almost every major denomination began setting their liturgies in a jazz idiom. Ed Summerlin, Ian Mitchell, Ray Repp, and John Ylvisaker each put their pen to the staff paper.

Since standard denominational hymnals are designed to last about a generation, supplemental paperback hymnals, carrying these new songs, were published. The Lutherans, for example, published at least three: 1967 *Hymns for Now: A Portfolio for Good, Bad or Rotten Times,* 1969 *Hymns for Now II,* and 1972 *Hymns for Now III.* These songs could be tried out—mainly with youth groups—and some judgments formed as to their durability and fitness for general congregational use. From such collections have come the following songs which are now published in major hymnals:

'Tis the gift to be simple (Shaker) (E45)
They'll know we are Christians by our love
Lord of the dance (RC128)
Every star shall sing a carol (RC74)
By the Babylonian rivers (RC38)

9, Copyright 1960 by Josef Weinberger Ltd., 33, Crawford St. London. An assessment of "Popular Music in the Church" appeared in an article with this title in *Church Music*, 69-2, a magazine published by Concordia Publishing House.

As we pointed out in Chapter 4, many hymn writers are now engaged in the expression of social and ecological concerns. Albert F. Bayly (1901-) is an English Congregational minister who has written over a hundred hymns. His best-known hymn in the United States is "Lord, whose love in humble service" (M479, L423). Here are three other Bayly hymns available in the *Lutheran Book of Worship:* "Lord, save your world" 420, "Lord of all, our gifts we bring" 411, and "Praise and thanksgiving" 409.

Fred Pratt Green (1903-) is an English Methodist clergyman and playwright who is considered one of the finest living hymn writers.[10] The following list of his hymns attest to his growing popularity:

This joyful Eastertide (B124)
When the church of Jesus (B319)
The first day of the week (L246)
O Christ, the Healer, we have come (L360)
The Church of Christ, in every age (L433)
When in our music God is glorified (L555)
For the fruit of all creation (L563)
Glorious the day when Christ was born (E63, RC91)
Christ is the world's light (E66)
God in his love for us (E75)
Rejoice with us in God (E101)

A Dutchman by birth, Fred Kaan (1929-) was on the staff of the World Council of Churches in Geneva. For some years now, he has been living in England where he is a United Reformed minister. One of his hymns "Today I live" was quoted with music on page 5. Dr. Kaan tells in an interview how he started to write hymns:

> It all started out of sheer necessity, because the whole, long, bitter process that came back with relentless regularity every week always included those moments of frustration when I couldn't find in the hymnal what I was really looking for. It was therefore out of frustration on the one hand, but also out of an eagerness and longing to find contemporary ways of singing the faith and "rejoicing in doctrine," that I began to write."[11]

10. See his article "Hymn Writing in Retirement" in *The Hymn*, October 1977.
11. See *The Hymn*, October 1980 for article "An Interview with Fred Kaan. (Copyright

Recent hymnal editors have become aware of Kaan's incisive-ness of language and insight of faith and have included a number of his hymns. For example, *The Hymn Book of the Ang-lican Church of Canada and the United Church of Canada* has 25 of his hymns! The Roman Catholic hymnal *Worship II* in-cludes twelve.

Here are a few samples:

Lord, as we rise to leave this shell of worship (E87)
As we break the bread (E60)
God who spoke in the beginning (E80)
Praise the Lord with joyful cry (E100)
For the healing of the nations (RC82)
God calls his people firm to stand (RC96)
We long to learn your praise (RC295)
Christ is crucified today (C104)
Now let us from this table rise (C97)

Brian Wren (1936–) is another minister in the English United Reformed Church who combines theological perception with a fresh expression of the implications of Christian faith in contemporary life.[12] Among his many hymns are the following:

Christ is alive! Let Christians sing (L363, E68)
Lord Christ, the Father's mighty son (RC165)
Christ, upon the mountain peak (E67)
Thank you, Lord, for water, soil and air (E78)
I come with joy to meet my Lord (E84)

The bibliography at the end of this volume concludes with a list of a dozen hymnals published in the last twelve years. Most of the significant recent hymns may be examined in these books.

A List of Hymn Tunes According to Types and Eras

These tunes are samples illustrating most of the major styles of hymn tunes. For a detailed analysis of hymn music, see Erik

---

© 1980 by The Hymn Society of America. Used by permission.) Most of Kaan's hymns are found in *Break not the Circle* (Carol Stream, IL: Agape, 1975), *Pilgrim's Praise* (London: Galliard, 1972), and *Worship the Lord* (Oakville, ONT: Harmuse Publications, 1977.
12. An interview with Brian Wren was carried in two issues of *The Hymn,* January and April 1981.

Routley's *The Music of Christian Hymns*, Revised Edition, published 1981 by GIA Publications, Inc.

Plainsong
Adoro Te Devote; Veni, Creator Spiritus; Divinum Mysterium; Veni, Emmanuel; Conditor Alme.

French Church Melodies
Deus Tuorum Militum; Christe Sanctorum; Solemnis Haec Festivitas.

Genevan Tunes
Commandments; Donne Secours; Old 100th; Old 124th.

German Tunes
Christ Ist Erstanden; Schmücke Dich; Quem Pastores; Ein Feste Burg; Nun Danket Alle Gott.

English and Scottish Psalter Tunes
St. Flavian; Winchester Old; Dundee; St. Anne; Hanover.

Victorian English Tunes
Aurelia; Nicaea; Lancashire; Diademata; Lauda Anima.

Twentieth-Century British Tunes
King's Weston; Sine Nomine; Mercer Street; Wylde Green; Birabus; Shillingford; Bridegroom; Hampton Poyle; Sharpthorne.

Welsh Hymn Tunes
Bryn Calfaria; Blaenhafren; Arfon; Aberystwyth; St. Denio.

Twentieth-Century American Tunes
Vineyard Haven; Geneva; New Dance; The King's Majesty. St. Dunstan's; Hinman; Christ Church; Fortunatus New.

Traditional Melodies
Bunessan; Greensleeves; Royal Oak; Wondrous Love.

Chapter VI

HOW TO UNDERSTAND AND USE YOUR HYMNAL

A hymnal is an anthology of hymns, to be used privately or publicly for devotional purposes by Christians. At least three trends can be traced in the hymnals of this generation. First, there has been a healthy move toward a core of hymnody, common to the major denominations. The ecumenical spirit in Christendom has been a major factor in this development. The list of basic hymns in the previous chapter is a graphic illustration of this fact. Second, most hymnals contain a more balanced representation of the mainstreams of church song, drawn from the major periods of church history, although as was noted in Chapter 5 we still draw the preponderance of our hymns from Victorian England. Third, where there is a distinctive denominational heritage in hymnody, this has been affirmed by generous inclusion of this type of music. For example, the *Lutheran Book of Worship* (1978) has an abundance of German and Scandinavian Lutheran texts and music. The Wesley brothers are represented by 85 hymns in the Methodist *The Book of Hymns* (1964, 1966), and the Presbyterian *The Hymnbook* (1955) contains eighty metrical psalms continuing the tradition initiated by John Calvin in the sixteenth century.

Thousands of different hymnals and psalters have been edited and their variety seems to be numberless. Some of them have had enormous circulation. The British *Hymns Ancient and Modern*, first issued in 1861, has had an estimated publication of over sixty million copies in its various editions. By contrast, Dr. Louis Benson's collection of his own *Hymns* (1925) was privately printed with three hundred copies. There is an old German hymn book *Evangelischer Liederschatz für Kirche, Schule, und*

Haus (1850) with 3,067 hymns in it whereas the Lutheran supplementary collection *Hymns for Now* (1967) has 26 songs. Most denominational hymnals are approximately the same size. However, the pocketsize French Evangelical Protestant hymnal *Louange et Prière* (1945) includes not only text but complete music. Even smaller is the little vest-pocket *Wayside Hymnal* (1940) published by the Episcopal Church at the beginning of World War II. The editors said, "A little book can make its way where a bigger—and worthier—may not at first go. We have made our book small, for the child's hand, for the pocket, the haversack, the dunnage bag, for the pillow; cheap enough for rough service and rough weather, for easy giving and sending."[1]

Most standard hymnals in America are denominational collections, edited and published officially by denominational boards specifically for use by congregations in these particular churches. However for use in multi-lingual gatherings, the polyglot *Cantate Domino* was prepared first by the World's Student Christian Federation in editions dated 1924, 1930, 1950, and 1974. The third edition (1950) contained 95 hymns with 83 appearing in German, 80 in English, 78 in French, and 47 in twenty other languages. Each hymn was presented in three languages. *Cantate Domino* (1974) was published by the World Council of Churches with editorial participation by the Roman Catholic and the Eastern Orthodox Churches.[2]

The first book printed in English America was *The Whole Booke of Psalmes Faithfully Translated into English Metre.* Called the Bay Psalm Book or New England version of the Psalms, it was printed at Cambridge, Massachusetts in 1640 by Stephen Daye.[3]

Some hymnals have interesting unique features. In *The Scottish Psalter 1929* the music of the psalm is at the top of the page and the text is at the bottom. Each page of the psalter is cut across the middle, like the old-fashioned barn door, so that it is

---

1. Published by Forward Movement Publications, 412 Sycamore Street, Cincinnati, OH 45202. (Copyright © 1940. Used by permission)
2. Kassel: Bärenreiter Verlag published the melody only edition in 1974. A full music edition of this hymnal was published in 1980 by Oxford.
3. See *The Bay Psalm Book. A Facsimile Reprint of the First Edition of 1640.* Ed. by Zoltan Haraszti. Chicago: University of Chicago Press, 1956.
   Also see *The Enigma of the Bay Psalm Book* by same author and press in 1956.

possible to have any text and music in the book presented on the
same surface. For example, tune #61 *French (Dundee)* could
be on the same page as Paraphrase #38 "Just and devout old
Simeon liv'd." The publishers of Hymns Ancient and Modern
issued a special edition of music without texts called *The Transposed Tune Book: The Tunes Transposed into a Lower Key Suitable for Unison Singing* (1939). Both *The Brethren Hymnal*
(1951) and the *Baptist Hymnal* (1975) have symbols located
above the music score which indicate to the organist or pianist
how the hymn may be shortened in playing over before the congregation begins singing. Several denominations (Methodist in
1966, Presbyterian in 1972 and Lutheran in 1978) have issued
worshipbooks which include not only a collection of hymns but
the complete liturgies for the various rites of the church. *The
Mennonite Hymnal* (1969) and the *Baptist Hymnal* (1975) are
published also in shape note edition. The *Lutheran Book of Worship* (1978) is issued in Braille as well as in large print for
visually handicapped persons. The full accompaniment edition
of *Ecumenical Praise* (Agape 1977) gives exact metronome in-
dications for each hymn.

Hymnal Prefaces

Be sure to read the preface of your hymnal. In addition to
giving the background of hymnals in your denomination, the
preface usually explains the principles which guided the editorial committee in its selection process and it frequently gives
directions for the efficient use of the book.

Hymnal Patterns

The hymns in most hymnbooks are arranged according to one
of the following two patterns:
1. *Topical grouping.* Many hymnals have the entire body
of hymns sorted and located according to a framework of doctrine, function, or occasion. Here is a typical pattern of contents
with the major headings. There are usually a number of hymns
listed under each subhead.
    Worship: Adoration and praise, morning, evening, the
        Lord's day, closing.

God:
   God the Father: eternity and power, in nature, love and
                   fatherhood, presence.
   Jesus   Christ: adoration and praise, advent, birth,
                   epiphany, life and ministry, triumphal en-
                   try, passion and atonement, resurrection,
                   ascension, presence, coming in glory.
   The Holy Spirit
   The Holy Trinity
   The Holy Scriptures
   Life in Christ: call of Christ, repentance and forgiveness, dis-
                   cipleship and service, dedication and consecra-
                   tion, stewardship, hope and aspiration, pil-
                   grimage and guidance, loyalty and courage,
                   trial and conflict, faith and assurance, love,
                   joy, peace, life everlasting.
   The Church: the Church, Lord's Supper, Holy Baptism, mar-
                   riage, Christian home, hymns for the young,
                   hymns for youth, Christian fellowship.
   The Kingdom of God on Earth: world friendship and peace,
                                   missions, city, nation.
   Miscellaneous: Dedication of a church, ministry, travelers,
                   thanksgiving, New Year.

   2. *The Church Year.* Denominations using a more liturgical form of worship (Episcopal and Lutheran) begin their book
with hymns arranged according to the Church Year. These are
then followed by hymns grouped around various topics. Here, for
instance, is the table of contents of the hymn section of the
Lutheran Book of Worship (1978):
   The Church Year: Advent, Christmas, Epiphany, Lent, Holy
                   Week, Easter, Ascension, Pentecost, The
                   Holy Trinity, Christ the King, Lesser Fes-
                   tivals.
   The Church at Worship: Holy Baptism, Holy Communion,
                   The Word, Beginning of Service,
                   Close of Service, Morning, Eve-
                   ning, Pastors, Marriage.
   The Life of Faith: Justification, Repentance, Forgiveness,

Christian Hope, Community in Christ,
Witness, Stewardship, Society, Prayer,
Trust, Guidance, Commitment, Praise,
Adoration, Celebration, Jubilation.

Two hymnals—*Christian Hymns,* published in 1963 by the
National Council of Churches of Christ in U. S. A., and *The
Worshipbook,* published by Presbyterians in 1972—have their
hymns placed alphabetically by first line titles.

Page format

Hymnals are generally published with full music score.
American hymnals ordinarily have most or all of the text between the music staves. When the editors believe that the hymn
should preferably be sung in unison, they print the melody line
above the text as is done in the hymn on the next page.
This hymn, taken from the accompaniment edition of *Ecumenical Praise* (Agape, 1977), presents a new musical setting for this
very familiar text. It will serve as an example of a hymnal page
format. Information about the source of the text is on the left
hand side at the top (sometimes this data is located at the bottom
of the page.) The Rev. Maltbie D. Babcock wrote the text. A
notation explains that stanza 3 was altered by Mary Babcock
Crawford. This was done undoubtedly to give opportunity for
congregations to express concern for ecology. Some hymnbooks
include after the author's name either the date of the hymn's
writing or the birth and death dates of the author. If the hymn
was translated from another language, the translator's name
and date are given and, sometimes, the title of the book containing the original text.
   Similar information about the origin of the music is given at
the right side of the page. In this case, Sir Malcolm Williamson
is the composer and he has named this melody *Mercer Street*
after a main street in Princeton, New Jersey.
   Under the title "This is my Father's world" are the initials S
M D. This is the abbreviation for Short Meter Doubled and its
meaning will be explained later in this chapter under the heading of Metrical Index.

This Is My Father's World

Maltbie D. Babcock
St. 3 alt. by Mary Babcock Crawford*

S.M.D.

Malcolm Williamson
Mercer Street

Slowly and gently ♩ = 72

1. This is my Fa - ther's world, And to my lis - tening ears All na - ture sings, and round me rings the mu - sic of the spheres. This is my Fa - ther's world: I rest me in the thought Of rocks and trees, of skies and seas His hand the won - ders wrought.

2. This is my Fa - ther's world, The birds their car - ols raise, The morn - ing light, the li - ly white, de - clare their Ma - ker's praise. This is my Fa - ther's world: He shines in all that's fair; In the rust - ling grass I hear Him pass, He speaks to me ev - ery - where.

3. This is our Fa - ther's world, O let us not for - get That though the wrong is great and strong, God is our Fa - ther yet. He trusts us with His world, To keep it clean and fair, All earth and trees, all skies and seas, All crea - tures ev - ery - where.

Also in hymnals where texts have been grouped according to categories, the editors will indicate either at the top or bottom of the page the title of the topical grouping, for example, "Morning Hymns" or "Christmas." This enables a leader of worship, in search of a hymn dealing with a given theme, to thumb through a section of related material and make an intelligent choice.

When editors do not have room to print an alternate tune on the opposite page and yet feel that one should be suggested, this advice is usually added as a footnote under the hymn.

Service Music

In addition to the main body of hymns, most denominational hymnals include additional congregational or choral service music. If the liturgies are printed in full, the responses, chants, acclamations, and canticles are inserted at appropriate locations.

Indexes

A variety of indexes is provided in most standard hymnals to permit efficient use of the contents. Here are the usual ones:

1. *Table of contents.*   Two sample tables were given earlier in this chapter.

2. *Index of first lines.*   In denominational hymnbooks the hymns are designated almost always by the first lines, except when there is a special title like "The Old Rugged Cross." The *Hymnal of the Moravian Church* (1969) has an "Alphabetical Index of First Lines of All Stanzas." In the *Lutheran Book of Worship* (1978) there is an asterisk by each hymn in its first line index which is included in the list prepared by the Consultation on Ecumenical Hymnody.

3. *Index of tune names.*   Every tune worth its salt has a name. There are many explanations for tune names. For example, a tune may be named after the first words of the hymn in its original language (*Lobe Den Herren* "Praise to the Lord, the Almighty" and *Ein Feste Burg* "A mighty fortress is our God" are examples.) The tune *Old 124th* has carried the text of the 124th Psalm. Sometimes the tune indicates a city or street associated with its composition, e.g. *Aberystwyth* and *Duke Street*. The tune *Beecher* ("Love divine, all loves excelling") was named for the famous Brooklyn minister, Henry Ward Beecher, whose

organist, John Zundel, composed it. Robert G. McCutchan's *Hymn Tune Names* (Abingdon Press, 1957) gives the background of most of our familiar hymn tune names.

4. *Metrical index.* For the uninitiated, this is the most complicated and intriguing index. Its purpose is to facilitate judicious exchange of tunes and texts of similar meter. In this index all tune titles which fit a particular metrical pattern are grouped together. We noted that the tune *Mercer Street* (page 78) has the initials SMD under the hymn title. Sometimes we see numbers like 76.76 next to the tune name. These numbers and abbreviations indicate the metrical framework of the text. In other words, these symbols tell the exact number of syllables per line or phrase. Since the tune of a particular text matches it line by line, it usually means that it is possible—and sometimes desirable—to exchange a text and tune which have the same metrical pattern.

To illustrate how this exchange can take place, recall the familiar Doxology text, "Praise God from whom all blessings flow." Each one of the four lines in this text has eight syllables in it and consequently has been called Long Meter 88.88. Look in your Metrical Index and you will find a list of tunes under the heading LM or Long Meter. Every one of these tunes will fit texts with eight syllables in each of its four lines although it may not be desirable to match all of them indiscriminately.

Under this heading of Long Meter we find the Doxology tune *Old Hundredth.* Also you will probably find such tunes as *Hursley* "Sun of my soul, thou Saviour dear," *Duke Street* "Jesus shall reign," and *Germany* "Where cross the crowded ways of life." Try singing the text "Sun of my soul, thou Saviour dear" with the Doxology tune *Old Hundredth* or sing the text "Praise God from whom all blessing flow" with the tune *Germany.* This kind of swapping may have a jarring effect.

The major use of this Metrical Index is to enable a leader of worship to substitute a familiar tune for the unfamiliar one printed in the hymnal. The leader knows that the people can read and understand any English text in the book but the leader recognizes that they may balk quite understandably at a tune which they have never sampled before. Perhaps on Thanksgiving day the leader desires to use William Pierson Merrill's stirring hymn whose first stanza is:

"Not alone for mighty empire stretching far o'er land and sea,
Not alone for bounteous harvests, lift we up our hearts to Thee.
Standing in the living present, memory and hope between,
Lord, we would with deep thanksgiving praise Thee most for things unseen."
(M548, L437, P512)

In many hymnals this text is wedded either to the Welsh tune *Hyfrydol* or to *Geneva,* a modern American melody. Suppose the congregation does not know either of these tunes and there is no time or opportunity to teach the people. The minister could use the text and find another tune known to the people. The metrical pattern of this text is 87.87.D (D means doubled, that is, 87.87.87.87.) In the Metrical Indexes of most hymnals there are at least a dozen tunes with this syllabic numeration. Tunes like *Converse* "What a friend we have in Jesus" (B403, M261, L439, P385) and *All The Way* "All the way my Saviour leads me" (B214, M205, P365) would be eliminated as not matching the mood of Merrill's text. The tunes *Hymn To Joy* "Joyful, joyful, we adore thee" (B31, M38, L551, P21) and *Austrian Hymn* "Glorious things of thee are spoken" (M293, L358, P434), might suit the text acceptably. By means of a note below this hymn, many editors suggest *Austrian Hymn* as a good alternate tune.

A brief study of a Metrical Index will reveal this simple arrangement. First are listed the Short Meter tunes which have the pattern 66.86. If this pattern is repeated in the same stanza, the category is listed as Short Meter Double or 66.86.66.86. Next comes Common Meter and Common Meter Double which are 86.86 and 86.86.86.86. This is followed by Long Meter which we described above. After these three major classes of meters— Short, Common, and Long—we find the remainder of the tunes listed in rising serial order. For example, this section might begin with 457.457 and refrain *Earth and all Stars* (L558, E73) and end with 15.15.15.6 and refrain *Battle Hymn Of The Republic* (B510, M545, L332)

Several bits of advice are offered regarding use of this method of tune interchange:

(A) If possible, use the tune given with the text. Follow some of the teaching procedures suggested in Chapters 14 if the tune is unfamiliar. It is stagnating always to revert to a few old and tried familiar tunes.

(B) When seeking a new tune, find a musical setting which

matches the mood and spirit of the text. One would never think of matching the text "O God our help in ages past" with the tune *Serenity* "Immortal Love, forever full" (B329, M158, P229) or the text "Once to every man and nation" with the tune *Bradbury* "Saviour, like a Shepherd lead us." (B213, M121, P380)

(C) The accentual pattern of the text and tune must match. For example, the text "Gentle Mary laid her child" (M395, P167) and the tune *Aurelia* "The church's one foundation" (B236, M297, L369, P437) are both 76.76.D and yet they will not match because their accentuation is reversed. The text has the accent on syllables 1-3-5-7 which is trochaic whereas the tune throws the accent on 2-4-6 which is iambic. In the Metrical Index of Episcopal *The Hymnal 1940* and Methodist *The Book of Hymns* 1964, 1966), groups 76.76.D and 87.87.D are separated into iambic and trochaic.

5. *Topical index.* This index lists the hymns under many subject headings. It is a valuable tool for a worship leader needing a hymn to develop or emphasize a particular theme. Since many hymns have a number of subordinate but important emphases, this index helps locate them. By way of illustration, in many hymnals the hymn "Joyful, joyful, we adore thee" is found in a section entitled Worship: Adoration and Praise. Nevertheless it has a strong nature emphasis. Therefore in many topical indexes this hymn may be listed also in the section of Nature Hymns.

6. *Index of authors, composers, and sources.* All authors and composers are listed alphabetically along with hymn number(s) designating the texts or music created by these persons. This index is handy if you have forgotten the title of a hymn but recall the author. Also if you desire to plan a special hymn service based, for example, on music by famous composers, this index is a useful tool for locating names like J. S. Bach, Beethoven, Mendelssohn, and Vaughan Williams.

7. *Other indexes.* There are a number of specialized indexes. Several hymnals include an Index of Hymns for the Church Year which suggests three or four hymns appropriate for each Sunday in the Christian year. An Index of Scriptural Allusions or References in Hymns is included in an increasing number of hymnbooks. The *Lutheran Book of Worship* has an index of *Original Language First Lines of Hymns.* It is interesting to note

that the hymns in this book originated in 20 languages other than English. Since a number of churches are following the three year lectionary, some editorial committees are preparing an index of hymns consonant with these readings from Scripture. The *Hymnal for Colleges and Schools* (Yale, 1956) has a unique set of brief background notes on each hymn.

Additional advice about hymnals: supply enough hymnals in the pews so that every church member can have a copy from which to sing. Stimulate members to purchase their own copies of the hymnal for home use.

Every student of hymnody should have at least one hymnal of superior quality even though it may not be one's own denominational book. here are a few titles generally considered in the top bracket:

The English Hymnal with Tunes (Oxford, 1906)
Songs of Praise with Music Enlarged Edition. (Oxford, 1931)
Worship II (G.I.A. Publications, Chicago, 1975)
Pilgrim Hymnal (Pilgrim Press, 1958)
Ecumenical Praise (Agape, 1977)
Lutheran Book of Worship (Augsburg, 1978)

Many additional hymnals are listed in the bibliography.

Chapter VII

THE MINISTER AND HYMN SINGING

The spiritual leader (whether minister, rabbi, or priest) has a crucial role in the development of strong congregational singing. The leader who knows the potential in hymns, who helps develop a long-range program of hymnic education, who selects hymns carefully and sings enthusiastically in the pulpit can be a powerful force in cherishing the spirit of song in his or her flock. The pastor's effectiveness as an enabler of hymn singing does not depend necessarily on musical talent and training, though these help when present.

In his Stone Lectures at Princeton Seminary in 1926, Louis Fitzgerald Benson (1855-1930) emphasized this pastoral responsibility by expressing it negatively: "There is a great deal of half-hearted and perfunctory singing in our services; an atmosphere of indifference or inattention from which it must be rescued. It was quite vain to deny that our pastors are to a considerable degree responsible for this. The indifference in the pews is very apt to be the reflection of the indifference in the pulpit."[1]

Hymn Appreciation. One way of increasing one's appreciation of hymnody is to make a habit of reading a hymn in daily devotions. The hymns of Thomas Ken (1637-1711), Charles Wesley (1707-1788), and Isaac Watts (1674-1748) are classics and a good starting place. And, if your hymnal was published recently, be sure to read contemporary hymn authors like Fred Kaan (1929-), Brian Wren (1936-), and Fred Pratt Green (1903-).

1. From *The Hymnody of the Christian Church,* p. 274. Richmond: John Knox Press, 1956.

Follow the custom of Phillips Brooks (1835-1893) and Dietrich Bonhoeffer (1906-1945) and memorize hymns. Ken's morning hymn "Awake, my soul, and with the sun" (M180, L269, P50) and his evening hymn "All praise to Thee, my God, this night" (B43, M493, L278, P63) and Neumark's "If thou but suffer God to guide thee" (B203, M210, L453, P344) are samples. This absorption of the spiritual essence of hymns will give strength to your liturgical and pastoral ministry.

James Muilenburg and Robert McAfee Brown are two examples of churchmen who were indebted to the power of hymns in their lives. Muilenburg, former Professor of Hebrew at Union Theological Seminary in New York City, said in a Lenten discussion at the Seminary:

> I should like to say something about the things that have influenced my life most deeply. First of all is the central importance of prayer. If there has been one continuous stream throughout my life, then it has been the awareness not only that there is a God, but that He is a God who hears. Closely associated with this is the continuing influence of the great hymns of the Church. It would not be difficult to speak of my spiritual pilgrimage in the language of the great hymns.[2]

Robert McAfee Brown, in his 1960 inaugural address at Union Theological Seminary in New York City, paid high tribute to hymns:

> If the real test of a theological affirmation is whether or not it can be sung—and that may be the most important test—then the affirmation of gratitude is a particularly resonant Protestant affirmation. And there is one hymn that more than any other expresses this Protestant stance of gratitude. It is a hymn that seems to be the appropriate hymn for every occasion of Protestant worship . . . It is the appropriate hymn to sing before or after a meal, and was in fact originally written to be sung as a grace. It is the hymn that I fervently hope will be sung at my funeral (let those here present take note, should any of you outlive me). It is the hymn that sums up what our reaction to the gospel must be, and describes what kind of people we must be because of the gospel. It is the hymn *Now Thank We All Our God.*[3] (B234, M49, L533, P9)

Hymn knowledge.   Obviously your first need is to understand the structure and to know the contents of your hymnal. The

---

2. *Union Seminary Quarterly Review,* Vol. XVII, No. 4. May, 1962, p. 292. (Copyright © by Union Theological Seminary in the City of New York. Used by permission.)
3. Ibid. Special issue, December 1960. pp. 81-82.

preface, indexes, table of contents, and page format are tools for
intelligent use of this book of praise. To know the contents, in-
vite your musician and some friends to begin with you a sys-
tematic exploration of the entire book so that you can become
acquainted with all of the hymns of exceptional quality.

If your hymnal has a handbook or companion with information about each hymn text and tune, establish the habit of reading the story behind the several hymns you choose for Sunday
worship. A minister friend of mine who had this custom told me
that he had acquired a large body of interesting and significant
hymnic information over a three-year span. If your denomination does not have a hymnal handbook, I suggest that you examine the list of handbooks, guides, and companions which are
listed at the beginning of the bibliography and purchase one. My
preference would be either Ronander and Porter's *Guide to the
Pilgrim Hymnal* or Stulken's *Hymnal Companion to the Lutheran Book of Worship.*

Here is one example of hymn origin information which il-
lumines the text. The hymn "If thou but suffer God to guide
thee" was written by George Neumark (1621-1681) who suffered
hardships during the Thirty Year's War (1618-1648). As a
young man, while on his way to study law at the University of
Königsberg, he was robbed by a band of thieves of all that he
possessed except a prayer book and a few coins sewed in the hem
of his garment. Forced to give up his plan to attend the university, he wandered in search of employment. Finally he received a
position as tutor in the home of a wealthy judge in Kiel. Over-
joyed at his good fortune, he wrote, "which good fortune coming
suddenly, and as if fallen from heaven, greatly rejoiced me, and
on that very day I composed to the honour of my beloved Lord
the here and there well-known hymn 'Wer nur den lieben Gott
lässt walten'; and had certainly cause enough to thank the Divine compassion for such unlooked for grace shown to me." Both
the text and tune were probably written at the same time in
1641.

In addition to studying the background of individual hymns,
increase your understanding of the broader aspects of church
music. Purchase *Music and Worship in the Church,* Revised and
Enlarged Edition, by Austin C. Lovelace and William C. Rice
(Abingdon, 1976). Not only does this expansive manual include

chapters on the minister's responsibilities with regard to worship and congregational music, but it also describes in detail all other aspects of music in the life of a congregation. See also *Key Words in Church Music* (Concordia Publishing House, 1978.

The choice of hymns. Your hymnal probably contains between five and six hundred hymns. If your congregation sings as many as 100 of these in the course of a year, it is exceptional. Since the responsibility for choice usually rests with the minister, which 50-100 hymns will you select? There are many criteria to guide you, among which are familiarity, quality, appropriateness for the moment in the service and the Sunday of the church year.

In a more particular way, ministers face the same problem in hymn choice that hymnal editors face in selecting approximately 600 hymns out of a reservoir of well over a half-million Christian hymns. The music editors of the *Pilgrim Hymnal,* Ethel and Hugh Porter, express the problem in the Music Preface to this hymnal:

> An editor learns in working on a hymnal how many factors influence the final choice of words and music, how many differing demands and tastes of the congregations have to be satisfied, how mighty a force 'association' is in the hymns we know and love to sing. At the same time he becomes more aware of the vast riches in hymnody and of the scant use made of these treasures by ministers, church musicians, and congregations. He knows that the substitution of a new hymnal for an old one can contribute to the enrichment of corporate worship only if those responsible for its use will explore its contents with an open, receptive mind, seeking to find not only their 'old favorites' but also to discover and learn to appreciate fine tunes hitherto unfamiliar to them.[4]

Just as these editors had to winnow a vast collection of hymns to produce a hymnbook, so the individual leader of worship by his or her intelligent choice of a single hymn completes this process, thus bringing the accumulated experience of Christendom to a focus in the act of worship.

Many ministers request the assistance of the musician in the hymn selection process, especially with regard to the music. I urge you to take the initiative in setting up weekly consulta-

4. Reprinted by permission of the publisher from the *Pilgrim Hymnal.* Copyright © 1958 by the Pilgrim Press.)

tions about the service music with your musician. Do not turn
the total responsibility of hymn selection over to the organist/
choirmaster.

Selection of the hymns sufficiently in advance enables the
choir director and choirs to be better able to lead the hymns and
perhaps to sing an anthem based on one of the hymns. The
organist can learn to play the music and perhaps can prepare a
hymn or chorale prelude on one of the hymns. If the text is
particularly desirable but the tune seems too difficult (and there
is not time or opportunity to teach it), then there is a mechanism
for substituting a more familiar tune.

Give your people the best hymns in your book but do this
using sound educational principles based on readiness, gradualness, and repetition. When all of this has been done, keep in
mind the wise words of Sir Walford Davies:

> ... the chooser of hymns as of every kind of music for popular use,
> needs to remind himself constantly that there are many kinds of
> good music; that in some of them the goodness is discernible only
> by the trained musician; in others by some sort of specialist; in yet
> others by the crowd—but only on thorough acquaintance. Finally,
> and happily, there is the kind of musical goodness that makes
> instant appeal to the untrained no less than to the trained musi-
> cian. The music of which this may be said is truly universal; it is
> enormous in quantity, and it embraces every type, from the sym-
> phony to the simple organ voluntary, from the oratorio to the Ang-
> lican chant. Popular musical education must begin with such
> things. Persons and organists with a taste for medieval melodies,
> Genevan psalm tunes, and German chorales are apt to forget that
> their liking for such things is usually the result of long familiarity
> or of special study. They must not expect their congregations to
> share their delight at once—if ever.[5]

The list of basic hymns in Chapter 5 is a good starting place for
hymn exploration.

In selecting hymns for a particular service of public worship,
ministers in a liturgical denomination (e.g. Roman Catholic,
Episcopal or Lutheran) will find guidance in a hymnal index for
de tempore hymns which means that they are proper for a particular Sunday or festival in the church year. See, for example,
the list of "Hymns for the Church Year" p. 470, in the *Ministers*

---

5. From *Music & Worship* by Walford Davies and Harvey Grace. p. 196. New York: The
H. W. Gray Company, 1935. Reprinted by AMS Press, New York.

Desk Edition of the *Lutheran Book of Worship* (1978). They are related to the three-year ecumenical lectionary. See also *A Handbook for the Lectionary* by Horace T. Allen, Jr. (Philadelphia: Geneva Press, 1980). This handbook has a list of hymns, chosen from three Presbyterian hymnals, which are appropriate for each of the lectionary lessons.

In the liturgically "free" churches, the minister should realize that the overriding principle in hymn selection is that the hymn should capture and express the thoughts and feelings of the congregation at that moment in the action of the liturgy. There should be no hymnic *non sequiturs* in the service. As Carl Schalk wrote: "Luther viewed the congregational hymn or chorale as an integral part of the *liturgy* and not merely as a general Christian song loosely attached to worship."[6]

This is why the Presbyterians in their *Worshipbook* 1972 have a "Guide for the Use of the Hymns." In this Guide they have a section devoted to the Service for the Lord's Day. In this Service there are a number of actions which need a congregational response in song. Therefore this Guide lists a number of hymns under headings like "After Confession and Pardon," "After Old Testament Lesson," "After Creed," "After Offering," and so on.

If the minister prefers to select a topic or theme for the service, then the various elements of worship can focus on this subject. Although this plan is possible, it is not necessary that the service be monothematic. The hymns can reflect the various emphases resident in the lessons and prayers.

Regarding the choice of stanzas, a good general rule is to sing the entire hymn. If it seems wise and necessary to shorten a hymn, care must be used in stanza selection. A hymn like "Come, Thou Almighty King" with each stanza devoted to a Person of the Trinity obviously loses its meaning if shortened. Of course, people would miss a stanza of "The Lord's my Shepherd." The Episcopal *Hymnal 1940* Preface states: "The Commission has indicated, by use of the asterisk, those stanzas in certain hymns which may properly be omitted without violating the sense." One example of the Commission's judgment is the placement of asterisks by stanzas 3 and 4 of "A mighty Fortress

6. *Hymnal Companion to the Lutheran Book of Worship.* p. 19. Philadelphia: Fortress Press, 1981.

is our God." Under no circumstance announce the singing of only
the first stanza of this hymn. If you do, you and the congregation
will leave the Devil in complete charge!

> For still our ancient foe doth seek to work us woe; his craft and
> power are great; and, armed with cruel hate, on earth is not his
> equal.

Recall that there are many single hymn stanzas which can be
utilized in worship to express praise and thanks at the presenta-
tion of the offering or as acclamations after saying a creed. In
addition to the familiar Doxology, "Praise God from whom all
blessings flow," there are several dozen final stanzas in most
hymnals which would be also appropriate. The Methodist *The
Book of Hymns* (1964, 1966) lists 22 in the Topical Index under
the title Doxologies.

It is a good idea to keep a record of the date of use of each
hymn. Some ministers do this in the margin of their desk hymnal copy. Another good way is to have a large wall chart lined
with squares (say 2 by 2 inches) for each hymn in the book
beginning with number 1 in the upper left hand corner. Under
the hymn title in each square, enter the date of usage of the
hymn (e.g. 2/24/80). Thus at a glance you can survey your progress in utilizing the resources of your hymnal.

The minister's leadership of hymns in the pulpit.   Since the
minister is usually in full view of the congregation, his or her
example of enthusiastic singing of the hymns can thaw out and
encourage many congregations. If the minister's chair is out of
sight of the congregation, move into full view during the singing. If there is a public address or broadcast microphone near the
minister during hymn singing, the operator can be requested to
reduce the volume or cut it off completely if desired, or to shift
the pickup to the choir microphone.

During Holy Communion, consider using communion hymns
or metrical psalms—sung by choir and congregation and listed
in the bulletin. Also the congregation may be urged to turn to
the Holy Communion section of the hymnal to read and meditate
on these hymns. The singing of metrical psalms during communion was a custom in John Calvin's order of service in Geneva.

Do not hesitate to give concise, illuminative comments about
the hymns in the service. These frequently prod the congrega-

tion into paying more attention to the words and help them sing more intelligently. Some ministers regularly insert paragraphs in the bulletin about the hymns and their backgrounds.

Sermons and prayers can be enriched and made more incisive by quotation of hymn phrases or stanzas. I recall an unusual sermon, divided into three sections of seven minutes each, with three carefully chosen hymns to collect and express the congregation's reactions at the end of each section. Purchase Austin Lovelace's pamphlet *The Use of Hymns* from the Hymn Society of America for additional ideas regarding use of hymns in worship.

Standing seems to be the preferred posture for hymn singing in most churches.

Also, in announcing portions of hymns, know the difference between *stanza* and *verse*. Webster says: "*Verse* is properly a single metrical line; a *stanza* is a combination or arrangement of verses. The use of *verse* for *stanza* is contrary to the best usage."

Hymns as counselling tools. Some ministers as they counsel their parishioners quote or suggest hymn stanzas which can give comfort and relieve anxiety. For example, the following stanza from "How firm a foundation" (B383, M48, L507, P369) is easily memorized and can be a means of grace in daily life:

> Fear not, I am with thee, O be not dismayed,
> For I am thy God, I will still give thee aid:
> I'll strengthen thee, help thee, and cause thee to stand,
> Upheld by my righteous, omnipotent hand.

An unusual and wonderful use of hymns in counseling was recounted by Joseph R. Sizoo. During World War II, Dr. Sizoo was host one evening at a servicemen's canteen in New York City. At one corner booth he found a young British sailor who was deeply disturbed. Sitting down beside him, Dr. Sizoo listened to the sailor's story of the disaster which recently had overwhelmed him.

The lad had been engaged to a British girl in his home town of St. Ives. During a five-day leave they were to have been married. Arriving with joyful expectancy at St. Ives, he found to his horror a gaping hole where his fiancee's home had been. The German bombers had been over. Her people, his people and Janie were gone.

While trying to comfort the lad, Dr. Sizoo discovered that the sailor used to sing in the choir when he was a child. His favorite hymn was "Lead, kindly Light." At Sizoo's suggestion, they began to sing it and the sailor's voice became stronger and deeper. Then together far into the night they quietly sang "Abide with me," "O God, our help in ages past," and many other hymns. After a long while they arose. Dr. Sizoo, looking into the eyes of the lad, asked, "Think you can sleep now?" "Yes, thank you, sir," he replied. Arm and arm, they walked out into the early morning.[7]

7. Adapted with permission from "Kindly Light" by Joseph R. Sizoo, August 1945 Reader's Digest. Copyright © 1945 by The Reader's Digest Assn., Inc.

Chapter VIII

THE PLAYING OF HYMNS

The hymn player can do more than any other person to develop great congregational singing. No one else has as much control of the vital processes of hymn singing. The very life of the music flows through his or her spirit and fingertips.

This fact should constitute a challenge to all church hymn accompanists to learn and apply the principles of good hymn playing. Many organists who play Bach and Brahms superbly seem to lack the sympathetic understanding necessary to stimulate congregational singing. Yet there are definite principles and instructions which, if understood and applied, will go far toward making a first-rate hymn player.

Firm Leadership

The congregation appreciates confident, firm, authoritative playing. Your people will soon learn to trust and respond to your leadership. By authoritative leadership, I do not mean barging through the hymn with no regard to where the people are at the moment. I have heard some organists play who seemed to have ear plugs which prevented their being sensitive to the movement of the congregational singers. This sensitivity enables an organist to know how to vary touch from legato to some detachment or marcato which could nudge the people and bring them into line.

Congregational accompaniment is not like playing for a skilled soloist. This soloist has a will which determines the speed, volume, accents, pauses, etc. A congregation has no musical will. This must be supplied by the player. Congregational

security and trust can be generated by attention to the following
suggestions.

Accurate Playing

Speaking of musical singing and playing, a writer once said
that we must live under law before we live under grace. First
learn to play accurately. Accuracy is the foundation stone of all
music making. Practice the hymn until all pitches are correct.
At the same time be sure that all time values are correct. The
use of a metronome is essential, especially for beginners. There
are three common errors in time values:

a. *failure to sustain long notes and to pull through dotted
notes.* A dotted half note becomes a half note in many tunes
like *St. Catherine* "Faith of our fathers." (B143, M151, L500,
P348) Clipping time from a note usually means starting the next
note prematurely and thus distorting the rhythm. In sustaining
a long note in a hymn tune, the beat of the pulse should be felt by
the player. The habit of thinking of all long notes as being made
up of several shorter notes tied together is most useful in developing sustained tone of proper length. For example:

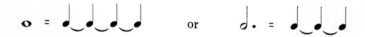

b. *tendency to clip rests.* Some players tend to ignore rests
in hymn tunes. Feel the pulse beat of the music right through
the silences.

c. *tendency to hurry eighth notes.* The first phrase of *St.
Margaret* "O love, that wilt not let me go" (B368, M234, L324,
P400) can trip many accompanists who fail to grasp the relation-
ship between the quarter and eighth notes. As a British writer
said, "The average singer [or pianist or organist] gets too much
pace on when the notes show tails."[1] For other examples, see
Serenity "Immortal Love, forever full" (B329, M158, P229) and
Converse "What a friend we have in Jesus." (B403, M261, L439,
P385)

---

1. Hugh S. Roberton, *Mixed Voice Choirs.* p. 4. London: Paterson's Publications, Ltd.,
   n.d.

Steady Beat

The remedy for the above time mistakes is the maintenance of a steady beat. Never stop the march of the song. The organist should count the time and visualize—or actually mark—the pulse beats above the score of each hymn. Then strive to maintain the rhythmic stride of the music. Frequent practice with a metronome, first slow, then progressively faster, will be an excellent aid in developing this accurate pulsation.

Nothing breeds confidence in a congregation's singing like a predictable schedule of regular beats at the console. Some 4/4 tunes like *St. Anne* or *Dundee* require a quarter note beat. Many others like *Lancashire, Nicaea,* or *Darwall's 148th,* though marked 4/4, maintain a better stride if felt and counted as 2/2 with the half note beat. This half note beat is especially important for maintaining the stride in many tunes which originated about the time of the Reformation. Many of these (*Es Ist Ein Ros, Psalm 42, Ein Feste Burg* rhythmic) have syncopations which are only apparent and musical with the half note beat. The *Lutheran Book of Worship* 1978 has removed bar lines from these tunes so that the horizons of the phrases are apparent from the start.

In a number of 3/4 tunes such as *Hyfrydol* and *Gelobt Sei Gott* it helps to maintain the stride by feeling a stronger beat on the first note of each measure.

Related to the subject of steady beats is the problem of handling fermatas which still appear in some hymnals. In some books these signs indicate a breathing spot, in others a pause. They should be played so that a steady pulse is maintained through the breathtime on the pause. The Lutheran book, mentioned above, wisely notates the exact time value between phrases in a tune such as the isometric *Ein Feste Burg*.

Play a ritard only at the end of the last stanza if at all.

Suitable Tempos

The speed of the beats varies from hymn to hymn. It is governed by the internal nature of the music, the emotion resident in the text, the acoustics and other factors. Since the determination of a suitable tempo is left to the hymn player, it helps to have no prejudice toward either slow nor fast tempos. Because some congregations tend to drag does not automatically call for rapid playing. Herbert Gotsch warns, "Younger or inexperienced organists for whom hymn playing offers no reading or coordination difficulties must especially guard against erring on the fast side in choosing tempos."[2]

In order not to be vague about this important subject, I list below the approximate metronome tempos of the singing of a few representative hymns in the album *A Time for Singing*.[3] (Q = quarter note, H = half note):
Duke Street H 80, *Sine Nomine* Q 120, *Lasst Uns Erfreuen* H 76, *Cwm Rhondda* Q 88, and *Ein Feste Burg* Q 84.

Organ articulation and touch

Rhythmic playing of hymns is largely controlled by articulation or touch at the organ. Rhythm is controlled and delineated by the release of the note as well as the attack.

Dr. Austin Lovelace in his excellent book *The Organist and Hymn Playing*[4] gives these specific rules for articulation in hymn playing.

1. Repeated notes in the soprano line are *always* broken to half their unit of value.

Aurelia

With a half note followed by two quarter notes, such as the beginning of "Fairest Lord Jesus," a dotted quarter note followed by an eighth note rest is the solution.

St. Elisabeth

2. *A Handbook of Church Music,* p. 193. (Copyright © 1978 by Concordia Publishing House.
3. See Item No. 9 in Chapter 1 for information about this album.
4. Revised edition, pp. 10–16. (Copyright © Agape, 1981. Used by permission.)

2. Repeated notes in the bass line are broken on the same principle of the unit of value, but whether to break or not is determined by a study of rhythmic and harmonic design. Repeated notes over the bar line are always broken because of the need for rhythmic impulse.

St. Anne

In any given measure repeated notes are broken if doing so adds to the life of the hymn.

Austrian Hymn

3. Repeated notes in the alto and tenor may generally be tied together except where more rhythm is needed or clarity is necessary in the inner voices.

Ratisbon

4. The beginning of a phrase on an upbeat calls for a complete break of half of the note value.

Irish

5. As a general rule both hands and feet should be lifted at the end of each musical phrase, at the places where the congregation takes a breath. This pause, or break, takes one half of a pulse and must be subtracted from the last note of the ending phrase note so that the forward movement is not halted.

6. Occasionally the words and punctuation may create the need to break all four parts. See, for example, the last phrase of the final stanza of "O worship the King all glorious above."

7. Cadences with dotted rhythms are usually broken in all voices to control the rallentando that can get out of hand with sluggish congregational singing.

8. In hymns where harmonizations are contrapuntally conceived, or where there are melodic motives which need to be heard clearly, the organist should articulate repeated notes in all voices. Bach harmonizations usually need this kind of treatment because of the interest in all parts.

9. All attacks should begin cleanly with hands and feet starting simultaneously. Many organists have the bad habit of putting down either the pedal note or the left hand first. Releases should likewise be clean, with no dangling pedal bourdons.

10. Articulation and touch are affected and partially determined by the acoustics of the room, the way the congregation sings, and most important of all, the form of the hymn.

Organ Registration

The registration will depend on the particular organ's resources but the usual combination will be principal or diapason tone at the 8', 4', and 2' pitches. Mixtures and reeds can be added on more vigorous hymns, stanzas, or phrases. In your selection of stops, do not be fussy. Omission of pedal on certain stanzas is permissible and some organists (for example, Fred Swann at the Riverside Church in New York City) drop the organ accompaniment entirely on certain stanzas and the effect of a vast congregation singing without accompaniment is thrilling.

The following two manuals will give more detail about the subject of registration and hymn playing in general:

Lovelace. *The Organist and Hymn Playing, Revised.* Ch. VII.
Halter and Schalk. *A Handbook of Church Music.* Ch. V. pp. 177–188.

Rhythmical Playing

The basis of all music is tonal movement. A competent organist does not move from chord to chord of the beautiful Irish tune *St. Columba* in picket-fence fashion, but rather moves through these chords and along the melody to certain points of climax and repose.

This music flows. In order to know where to move in a hymn tune, the organist should know the architecture of the total melody and the shape of phrases within this tune.

Intervals Between Stanzas

Organists should extend the last chord of a stanza somewhat to allow for a breath (and perhaps a swallow.) The hands are then lifted from the keys for a beat and then the new stanza is begun. A congregation will soon get used to the timing of this inter-stanza interval. The writer makes an exception to this rule in playing *Sine Nomine* "For all the saints." He holds the last chord for four beats and moves directly to the springboard pedal entrance to the next stanza, or the first three notes of the tune can be played in the pedals to keep the pace moving.

Amens

If amens are sung at the conclusion of hymns, they should be played in the mood and tempo of the hymn as it is finished. Many organists hold over the note which is common to the last chord of the stanza and the first chord of the amen. This sounding bridge signals to the people that the amen is to be sung.

Reading the Hymn Text

By studying the hymn text beforehand, the player can determine the organ registration, the tempo, the kind of touch, and the general mood from stanza to stanza. Then, while playing, read the text as well as the music. It will help in phrasing the music judiciously so that the congregation can sing more intelligently.

Introducing the Hymn

Before you touch the keys, establish mentally the pace at which you are going to play. Announce the hymn at the same tempo you expect the congregation to sing. Do not ritard at the end of this introduction. If the hymn melody is unfamiliar, play it all the way through. If it is familiar, many organists abbreviate the organ introduction of the music. By a series of bracket symbols, the *Baptist Hymnal* (1975) indicates how its hymn introductions can be abbreviated.

Organ intonations may be used to introduce hymns. These are brief compositions giving a part of the melody, establishing the tempo, and setting the mood of the hymn. Augsburg Publishing House has published a series of 15 packets of intonations and varied harmonizations of a number of hymns. They are titled *Hymn Preludes and Free Accompaniments.* Code numbers 11-9397 to 9411.

The use of chorale and hymn preludes are valuable aids in enriching worship and hymn singing.

Variation Methods of Hymn Accompaniment

A number of publishers have issued collections of alternate harmonizations to hymn tunes. Used discreetly (not overdone) and with prior explanation to the congregation, they can add color and excitement to congregational singing. Here are some titles:

Gerre Hancock *Organ Improvisations for Hymn-Singing,* Hinshaw HMO-100
Dale Wood *New Settings of Twenty Well-known Hymn Tunes,* Augsburg 11-92929
Theodore Beck *Forty-seven Hymn Intonations* Concordia 97-5018
Theodore Beck *Intonations on Selected Hymns* Concordia 97-5392

David N. Johnson *Free Hymn Accompaniments for Manuals* Books I and II. Augsburg 11-9185 and 11-9186

David N. Johnson *Free Harmonizations of Twelve Hymn Tunes* Augsburg 11-9190

Paul Bunjes *New Organ Accompaniments for Hymns* Concordia 97-5348

Paul G. Manz *Ten Short Intonations on Well-known Hymns* Augsburg 11-9492

T. Tertius Noble *Fifty Free Organ Accompaniments to Well-known Hymn Tunes* J. Fischer and Bro. 8430

Robert Scoggin *Festival Hymn Introductions.* Fortress 3-61

Chapter IX

THE CONDUCTING OF HYMNS

Although most congregations look to the keyboard for hymn leadership, there are occasions when a director needs to stand in front of a group and lead the singing with gestures. Since the Mennonites as a rule do not have instrumental accompaniment of hymns, they provide a person who gives the pitch and directs the unaccompanied hymn singing. The Southern Baptists also frequently have a precentor or song leader to guide congregational singing, even though they generally employ both organ and piano. There are many informal occasions when skill in direction of singing is useful, such as church supper hymn sings, church conferences, and outdoor vespers.

The precentor should possess a love of singing, be enthusiastic, have a reasonably good voice, and have the knack of encouraging everyone to participate. These leaders could manage without any knowledge of standard conducting patterns, giving mainly the pulse of the music and perhaps some indication of the pitch, the volume and emotion of the hymn.

However, they would get better results if they used standard conducting patterns. Three diagrams will show the ones which will enable you to conduct most of the usual hymns. Before displaying them, we should say that conducting is the complete expression of the music. It is foolish to expect the hand alone to accomplish this task. The entire person—body, mind, and spirit—is involved in this manifestation. The graceful movement of arms, hands and fingers; the strength and mobility of stance; the carriage of body and head; the expressiveness of countenance especially—all of these must be involved in conveying the emotions and words of the texts, the contours of the melody, the tempo, and the behavior of the rhythms.

102

The following conducting patterns have been accepted as conventional throughout the civilized worlds. In barest form they are designed to indicate the temporal progress of the music. Since music is a time art, one of the main points of reference as the music progresses is the periodic recurrence of a pulsation of time. These beats must be signaled to the singers in order that simultaneous progress can be made. For centuries these pulsations have been grouped in units of two, three, or four, or more beats (variations of duple or triple), and there are gestural patterns to show each set.

Four-Beat Gesture

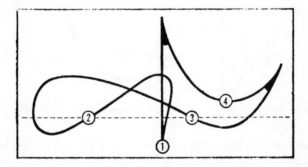

If you are right-handed, enlarge this pattern in your mind and practice this gesture in front of your body until it becomes automatic. The size of the gesture will be determined somewhat by the size of the group you are conducting and the distance you are from them. Practice this in private standing in front of a mirror, conducting while singing a 4/4 hymn like "Holy, Holy, Holy, Lord God Almighty" or "For the beauty of the earth." Do this until it becomes habitual. Now try tapping the rhythm of the melody with your feet while you sing and direct with your hand. Let your wrist be supple and flexible but portraying strength. Watch some topnotch orchestral conductors on television. If you want more accent in the singing, your beat can indicate this *marcato* and firmness. Develop your own style but try to eliminate distracting mannerisms. Don't be afraid to ask for comments from sensible friends.

If the hymn begins with a fourth beat (an anacrusis) like the tune *Aurelia*, "Lead on, O King Eternal" or *Nun Danket*, "Now thank we all our God," you would begin with the fourth beat of the pattern displayed above. The speed of this attack beat will indicate the pace you want for the entire hymn. If you are left-handed, reverse the movement on the second, third, and fourth beat.

Three-Beat Gesture

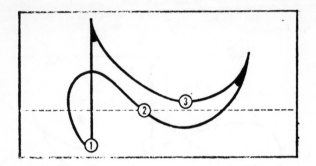

Note that the hand moves to the right for the second beat of this pattern as contrasted with the leftward motion of the second beat of the 4/4 pattern. Try this pattern with tunes like *Italian Hymn*, "Come, thou almighty King" and other 3/4 tunes. If the hymn is to have sprightly movement, then you may wish to give only one beat for the first note of each measure. The hymns "Immortal, invisible, God only wise" (*Joanna*) and "Good Christian friends, rejoice and sing!" (*Gelobt Sei Gott*) illustrate this stride.

Two-Beat Gesture

This beat pattern could be used with a number of 4/4 hymn tunes whose basic pulse should be indicated by 2/2. And some hymnals do show 2/2. In other words, tunes like *Duke Street*, "Jesus shall reign," *Lancashire*, "Lead on, O King eternal," and *St. Gertrude*, "Onward, Christian soldiers" can be better sung when a half note is the basic beat.

There are also a number of 6/8 tunes like *In Dulci Jubilo,* "Good Christian men, rejoice," and *Greensleeves,* "What child is this" which move with two fundamental beats on the first and fourth beats and thus should have this two-beat gesture.

Two-Beat Gesture

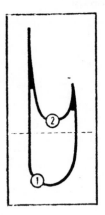

After you thoroughly learn these three patterns, feel free to alter them according to the needs of the music and the group. For example, in teaching a new melody, phrase by phrase, you may wish to indicate the rise and fall of melody by raising and lowering your directing hand or finger. This will enable amateurs to control the pitch of their voices and to learn the tune more easily.

Attack

When the group is ready to begin singing a hymn, hold your directing hand in front of you for attention. Then breathe (inhale) as you lift your hand. Then move right into the singing with the downbeat. We referred above to certain hymns which begin on the last beat of a measure. In starting a group singing these hymns, hold your hand in front of you and, as you inhale, move your hand up and to the right and away from your body. Then sweep your hand onto the path of the fourth beat shown in the 4/4 pattern and your group will be on its way.

Release

The release or stop is shown by a number of different motions. Usually a twist of the wrist, after the final note has been held long enough, will indicate the instant you expect the group to stop. An alternate way is to close the thumb and index finger to indicate the final consonant.

Chapter X

CHOIRS AND HYMN SINGING

The primary functions of the choir are to join with all other members of the congregation in offering worship to Almighty God and to lead the congregation in worship through hymns, anthems and the sung portions of the liturgy. The choirs, therefore, are committees of the congregation charged with responsibility for the music of the service of worship. Although the singing of anthems and "special" music is important, the prime responsibility of the choirs is the leadership of congregational singing.

The choirs, after all, are composed of people who are more confident of their singing ability and read musical notation reasonably well. They enjoy singing. They have opportunity for regular instruction. For these reasons, they can be musical shepherds of the flock. Here are several ways they can help.

1. Members of the choirs should give an enthusiastic visual and audible example of participation in the singing of hymns. By their vocal and facial expression they can stimulate the people in the pews to imitate them. The choir members are frequently in full view of the congregation, and the choristers' interest in and enjoyment of the hymns will be readily apparent.

2. They can encourage the congregation to sing by expressing interest and commendation when they mingle with the congregation in daily contacts. Most of the choristers have families in the pews and it helps for a more expert singer to commend and reinforce a layperson on an honest attempt at singing a new hymn.

3. Many childrens' choirs have hymn study projects.[1]

---

1. The Choristers Guild publishes hymn study sheets. They can be ordered from the Choristers Guild, P. O. Box 38188, Dallas, TX 75238.

Notebooks devoted to hymn stories and pictures are compiled. Quizzes of hymn facts are given. Stanzas are memorized and sung for the director or a "listening committee." See Chapter 13 for description of this plan. The educational values of these projects feed into the leadership of worship given by the childrens' choirs.

4. The choirs can help teach an unfamiliar hymn. Since the choirs can rehearse and master a new tune, the members are quite able to outline the melody and guide the people as they attempt to traverse a new tune. One of the best ways is to have all the choir singers sing only the melody, at least on the first and last stanzas. The melody is the path along which most of the congregation will try to move, and if it is clearly delineated by all the choristers, then the congregation will be reassured and helped.

John Calvin was faced with the problem of introducing new metrical psalm texts and new melodies to his Genevan congregations. He wrote: "This manner of proceeding seemed specially good to us, that children, who beforehand have practised some modest church song, sing in a loud distinct voice, the people listening with all attention and following heartily what is sung with the mouth, till all become accustomed to sing communally."[2]

5. The choirs can teach a new hymn by singing it first as an anthem. Hymns, when arranged skillfully, make beautiful and impressive anthems. What is more, they constitute an economical source of special choral music, for the material is instantly available in any good hymnal. The secret lies in arranging the hymns in interesting and appropriate ways so as to bring out the beauties inherent in the harmony and melody and in order to interpret effectively the meaning of the text. For the average choir to sing all five stanzas of a hymn in straight four-part harmony would be monotonous, to say the least.

Here is a list of twelve ways of varying the singing of certain stanzas or parts of stanzas of hymns:

a. All voices singing full harmony (accompanied or unaccompanied.

2. *Calvin: Theological Treatises.* Vol. XXII, p. 54. (Copyright © 1954 by Westminster Press.)

b. All voices singing melody only (unison.)
c. Men singing melody alone.
d. Women singing melody alone.
e. Solo voice singing melody accompanied by choir humming the harmonies. If no soloist is available, have the entire soprano section sing the solo, striving for clear blended tones and crisp diction.
f. Altos, tenors, and basses singing melody with sopranos singing a descant. If your hymnal does not have descants, you should order several collections. Using some of them as models, you might try your hand at writing some.

The Descant Hymn-Tune Book by Geoffrey Shaw. Vols. I and II, Novello.
Trumpet Hymns and Descants by Douglas Smith. Hope Publishing Company. No. 706

g. Sopranos and tenors singing their parts as a duet if these two voice parts are harmoniously arranged. See, for example, *St. Columba.*
h. Men singing the melody, altos their own part, and sopranos singing the tenor part an octave higher. Try this on one stanza of "Once to every man and nation."
i. A quartet, trio, or duet of solo voices.
j. A solo voice or section singing the melody with varied harmonization of accompaniment. See Chapter 8 for list of collections of alternate hymn harmonizations.
k. One or more stanzas sung in parts by men alone or women alone. There are a number of collections of hymns arranged for either of these vocal groups. Here are two suggestions:

Women: The Morning Star Choir Book, Ed. by Thomas. Concordia 97-6287
Men: The TTBB Chorale Book edited by Theodore Hoelty-Nickel. Concordia 97-7602

l. Modulation to a higher or lower key.
m. Changing from major to minor or reverse (e.g. *Arfon, Llangloffan*)

Among the many beautiful hymn tunes found in our major books, here are a few which would make splendid anthems. Try your hand at arranging them. Do not make the arrangements too elaborate and be sure that your choir members know the plan thoroughly:

Arfon, Innsbruck, Jesu, Meine Freude, BrynCalfaria, King's

Weston, Bunessan, Kingsfold, Christe Sanctorum, Llangloffan, Durrow, Es Ist Ein' Ros, O Gott, Du Frommer Gott, Sine Nomine, Walsall, Forest Green.

Here are a few titles of hymn anthems from among hundreds which could be suggested. Study them as models of skillful hymn arrangement:

Picardy "Let all mortal flesh keep silence"
         Carlton Young, Agape AG 7156.
         Gustav Holst, Galaxy 5.
         Donald Busarow, Augsburg 11-1844.

Old Hundredth "All people that on earth do dwell"
         R. Vaughan Williams. Oxford University Press.

Joanna "Immortal, invisible, God only wise" Eric Thiman, Novello, 1140.

Aberystwyth "Jesu, lover of my soul" Parry-Coleman, Oxford E45

Ratisbon "Christ whose glory fills the skies" Healey Willan, Concordia HA 2006

St. Columba "The King of Love my shepherd is" Edward Bairstow, Oxford A 46

Slane "Be thou my vision" Alice Parker, Hinshaw Music Co. HMC-135 Carlton R. Young, Neil A. Kjos, 5254.

King's Weston "At the name of Jesus" R. Vaughan Williams, Oxford 40-100

Down Ampney "Come down, O love divine" Dietterich, Hope Publishing Co. APM-241

Crusader's Hymn "Fairest Lord Jesus" Alice Parker/Robert Shaw Lawson-Gould 752

Christe Sanctorum "Father, we praise thee" R. Peek, Brodt 519

Deo Gracias "O love, how deep, how broad, how high" Carl Schalk, Concordia 98-1524

Here are three collections of hymn anthems:

Hymns for Choirs arranged by David Willcocks. Oxford University Press.

Gloria Deo: Easy anthems for Soprano, Alto, and Baritone. David Johnson. Book One, Augsburg 11-9160.

American Folk Hymns for Junior Choir. Arranged by Austin Lovelace. Carl Fischer, Inc., CM 7311.

The above anthems utilize the familiar melodies usually associated with these texts. The following titles employ many familiar texts but have new musical settings. Sung as anthems with the congregation following the text in their hymnals, new and fascinating dimensions open up to the worshippers:

Five hymns in popular style, John Gardner. Oxford
Choirbook for Saints and Singers, edited by Carlton Young, Agape, No. 939.
Ecumenical Praise, executive editor, Carlton Young. Agape.

A number of well-known hymns have been arranged in elaborate style utilizing congregation, one or more choirs, organ, and various instruments, usually brass. Here are some samples:

"Praise to the Lord, the Almighty, the King of Creation"
A Chorale Concertato by Paul G. Bunjes. Concordia 97-4450.
"Now thank we all our God" Alice Parker, Carl Fischer.
"The Church's One Foundation" Paul Manz. Concordia 97-4670.
"A Mighty Fortress Is Our God." David N. Johnson. Augsburg 1441
"Wake, awake, for night is flying" Harald Rohlig. Concordia 97-4670.

A cantata-length choral work utilizing eight hymns was composed by Lloyd Pfautsch entitled *Seven Words of Love,* (Hope Publishing Co.). The title is based on a phrase from Frederick Faber's hymn "O come and mourn with me awhile." This Faber text is the opening hymn in the cantata. Then each of Jesus' words from the cross is presented. First, the biblical passage is read and is followed by a choral setting of the particular word. Next a brief commentary on the passage by a famous theologian is read and finally the congregation responds by singing a hymn, usually a familiar one.

Chapter XI

THE PRIVATE USE OF HYMNS

The central spring of hymnody is in the heart of the individual Christian as he or she is moved by the Holy Spirit. Each person must ponder and absorb in private the meaning of the hymns before great congregational singing can be achieved. Louis Benson wrote: "It is only the precedent appropriation of the hymn's message by each individual heart that makes its congregational singing worthwhile."[1] Much of the meaning of a hymn will remain unfathomed if we depend on congregational singing alone to reveal the content. During ordinary hymn singing, the syllables and words pass before the consciousness at a speed of a second or less per word or syllable. We cannot fully grasp the relationship and sequence of ideas at this speed.

How many persons, for example, know what this phrase from "Rock of Ages" means: "Be of sin the double cure"? The next phrase tells us—cleansing from sin's *guilt* and *power*. Granted that most skillful hymn writers attempt to make their meaning very evident, we do have hymns which require considerable reflection before their full meaning can be discerned. For example, some recent hymnals (Presbyterian *The Worshipbook* 1972, p. 413 and *Ecumenical Praise* 1977, p. 72) include W. H. Auden's (1907-1975) poem "He is the Way". This hymn is rich in meaning but this is unfolded only by leisurely contemplating such phrases as "Follow Him through the Land of Unlikeness" and "Seek Him in the Kingdom of Anxiety."

To assist Christians to cultivate the habit of reading hymns, Erik Routley prepared *A Panorama of Christian Hymnody* which is a collection of 593 excellent hymn texts (no music) and

---

1. *The Hymnody of the Christian Church,* p. 228.

a number of articles or essays on aspects of hymnody. Professor
Routley states the first purpose of this volume as follows:

> The first purpose of the book is to provide pleasure, a pleasure
> which I discover to be now wholly hidden from those friends in
> America whom I admire and love so much as to wish to share it
> with them. That is the godly and sensible pleasure of *reading*
> hymns. I do not mean reading them communally in church, which
> strikes me as a miserable substitute for that cheerful song which is
> now the delight of all Christian communions. I mean reading them
> in solitude, reading them as lyric poetry.... When I remember how
> in my own youth, say thirty years back, men and women in so
> many branches of the church in England, my home country, would
> read their hymnals as eagerly and regularly as they read their
> Bibles, and would, if whipped off to hospital, reach for the hymn
> book as well as the Bible, I simply grieve to think that this particu-
> lar pleasure and religious nourishment is withheld from so many
> or ignored by so many in these later days.[2]

Seize the many opportunities for reading hymns. With your
own copy of your hymnal on your bedside table, you could either
read through the hymnal consecutively or select hymns which
fit your need at the moment. The Topical Index will help you. It
is interesting to note that the Third Edition of *The Church
Hymnary*[3] (1973) has Section VIII of more than thirty hymns
labeled "Personal Faith and Devotion," obviously designed
primarily for personal use.

Then do not neglect the few minutes during the Sunday morning prelude. Discover what hymns are to be sung in the worship
and read them beforehand. You will be able to sing with greater
insight and, as St. Paul said, "with understanding."[4]

Remember also that hymns can be *sung* in private. Bishop
Thomas Ken (1637–1711) wrote "Three Hymns for Morning,
Evening and Midnight" for the schoolboys of Winchester College. Each concluded with the familiar "Praise God from whom
all blessings flow." Ken advised the scholars: "Be sure to sing
the Morning and Evening Hymn in your chamber devoutly, re-
membering that the Psalmist, upon happy experience, assures
you that it is a good thing to tell of the loving-kindness of the

---

2. Published by The Liturgical Press. (Copyright © 1979 by the Order of St. Benedict,
   Inc., Collegeville, Minnesota. Used by permission.)
3. London: Oxford University Press, 1973. Nos. 663-695.
4. I Corinthians 14:15.

Lord early in the morning and of his truth in the night season."[5]
Ken's biographer, Dr. Hawkins, commented that Ken used to
sing his Morning Hymn to his lute daily before he put on his
clothes.

Those Christians who have leisurely pondered hymns will find
the opening lines of William Cowper's hymn true:

> Sometimes a light surprises the Christian while he sings;
> It is the Lord, who rises with healing in his wings.

---

5. *Manual of Prayers for the Use of the Scholars of Winchester College.* 1674 Edition.

Chapter XII

HYMNS IN THE FAMILY CIRCLE

In 1557, twenty-one years after John Calvin settled in Geneva, a visitor to that city recorded the following account:

> A most interesting sight is offered in the city on the weekdays, when the hour for the sermon approaches. As soon as the first sound of the bell is heard, all shops are closed, all conversation ceases, all business is broken off, and from all sides the people hasten to the nearest meeting-house. There each one draws from his pocket a small book which contains the psalms with notes, and out of full hearts, in the native speech, the congregation sings before and after the sermon. Every one testifies to me how great consolation and edification is derived from this custom.[1]

The Genevans took their psalter to church but it returned with them to their homes and daily lives. Today the hymnal is apt to remain in the church pew racks with the admonition sometimes printed on the flyleaf DO NOT REMOVE FROM THE PEWS.

Church members should be able to purchase a copy of their own denominational hymnal. Suggest that the church office stock sufficient copies for sale to the congregation. Publishers supply optional binding colors for this purpose and such hymnals also make excellent gifts. For example, if a child memorizes each of the Hymns of the Month (or one stanza of each), he or she could be given a hymnal engraved with his or her name.

The hymnal also belongs in the homes where individuals and families can read and sing and play and learn the hymns. One

---

1. Recounted in Millar Patrick's *The Story of the Church's Song,* p. 92. Richmond: John Knox Press, 1962. American Edition.

writer, speaking of Luther, said that he took hymns out of the liturgies and put them into people's hearts and homes, that when they had learned them and loved them, they might bring them to the church and sing them together.

Realizing the importance of family singing of hymns, the Lutherans have published a 64-page paperback hymnal called *The Hymn of the Week: A Songbook*. In its preface, the editors state: "Good hymn singing in a congregation is closely related to family singing. Actually a congregation is a larger Christian 'family,' when many families come together for worship. Hymns learned and sung at home will be sung much better when the larger family assembles in church."[2] To accompany this little hymnal, they have issued a three-record album called *A Time for Singing*. A family could learn each of these hymns by using this album.

Sabin Bonhoeffer Leibholz, a twin sister of the theologian, Dietrich Bonhoeffer, described their family singing of hymns:

> Christmas Eve began with the Christmas story. We sat in a big, family circle (the servants in white aprons were with us), all festive, waiting for our mother to begin to read. I shall never forget her in her black velvet dress with the beautiful point-lace collar, with her heavy, dark-yellow braids around her head, and below them her broad, serious forehead. Like many blue-eyed people, she had a very white skin, but it was rosy then with the joy of the festival. She read the Christmas story in a clear, full voice. All traces of overweariness and strain from her Christmas preparations—they reached far beyond the family circle—seemed to have vanished with the coming of the Holy Night. After the Christmas story she always started the song, "This Is the Day Which the Lord Has Made." I remember that the tears sometimes came to her eyes at the verse:
>
> > If I would grasp this wonder
> > My spirit would in awe stand still;
> > In adoration, too, would ponder
> > The love that God unending wills.
>
> And so also at the words of the Christmas story, 'But Mary kept all these things and pondered them in her heart.' Dietrich and I confided to each other that those tears troubled us very much and oppressed us, and that it was a relief when Mama's eyes were clear again.
>
> Now the light was put out and in darkness we sang Christmas

2. Copyright © 1965 by Augsburg Publishing House.

carols until our father, who had quietly left the room, had lighted
the candles by the crèche and on the tree. When the 'Christchild'
rang the bell, we three youngest could go to the lighted tree. There
we sang enthusiastically 'The Christmas Tree Is the Most Beautiful Tree.' Only after that did the distribution of gifts begin.[3]

Here are a number of ways in which families can utilize the
hymnal. Like the Bonhoeffers, they can sing hymns at festive
occasions. John Foster Dulles, former United States Secretary of
State, sang hymns with his family, especially at their summer
home. His favorite hymn, incidentally, was "Through the night
of doubt and sorrow" which was recorded for him in his terminal
illness by the student body of the School of Sacred Music at
Union Theological Seminary in New York City. This was played
for him in his hospital room.

Many families frequently sing a hymn stanza, or a portion of
one, as a blessing or grace at mealtime. "Now thank we all our
God" was written by Martin Rinkart as a mealtime blessing.
Just the first line of this hymn could be a starter for the family.
The familiar "Praise God from whom all blessings flow," "For
the beauty of the earth," and "Fairest Lord Jesus" are other
suggestions. Our family sings the familiar text "God is great,
God is good, and we thank him for this food" to this first line of
the folk hymn tune *Boundless Mercy:*

God   is   great and   God   is   good, and   we   thank Him   for   this food.   A - men.

Fathers and mothers often tuck their children into bed with a
prayer and a hymn. These hymns will ever afterward be associated with the dependency and trustfulness of early childhood. Sabine Leibholz listed her and Dietrich's favorite childhood hymns (among them, "Praise Ye the Lord" and "Now
Thank We All Our God") and describes how they sang them in
their nursery as they were tucked in bed. She says: "For the
evening singing we were allowed to choose the hymns, but if we

---

3. *Union Seminary Quarterly Review.* Vol. XX, No. 4. May 1965. pp. 326-327. Article
"Dietrich Bonhoeffer: A Glimpse into our Childhood." (Copyright © 1965 by Union
Theological Seminary in the City of New York. Used by permission.)

hesitated too long, our mother made the choice herself. She knew all the verses of most of the hymns by heart."[4]

If any of the children are taking lessons on the piano or other instruments, their teachers can be encouraged to include hymn music in their training. The church needs an ample supply of capable pianists and many leaders make church pianos available for practice during the week.

From time to time, the church bulletin or newsletter can carry some of the suggestions enumerated above. Dr. Louis Benson sums up the matter in this manner:

> "So inspiring and uplifting can the spiritual ministry of poetry and music to human lives be made that I venture to propose this task and opportunity of getting the hymnal back into the homes and hands and hearts of Christian people as one of the most rewarding that can engage us."[5]

4. Ibid. p. 324.
5. *The Hymnody of the Christian Church.* p. 276. Richmond: John Knox Press, Reprinted 1956.

Chapter XIII

HYMNS IN THE EDUCATIONAL PROGRAM OF THE CHURCH

In a long-forgotten hymnal the Reverend Archibald Alexander, first professor in Princeton Seminary, wrote the following prefatory words:

> Christians retain in their minds more of the gospel in the words of the spiritual songs which they are accustomed to sing than in any other form, and children can perhaps be taught the truths of religion in this way, more effectually than in any other ... the understanding is reached with most certainty through the feelings of the heart.[1]

Expressed in modern terms, cerebral learning must be reinforced by affective impressions. Also, nowadays, when we think of the educational program of the church, we know that it should be *continuing education.* We provide opportunities for everyone in the congregation to continue learning as long as earthly life is maintained.

The quality of hymn singing in the public worship of a congregation is determined largely by the hymnody employed in the church school. A less formal atmosphere, smaller groups, a teaching environment, intimate contact with concerned teachers, impressionable early years—these factors make it important that training in hymn singing be of high calibre in the church school.

The Need for a Single Standard in Hymnody

It is well nigh fatal to hold one standard in the more formal church worship and then "let the bars down" in the church

1. *A Selection of Hymns, adapted to the devotions of the closet, the family, and the social circle.* New York: Leavitt, 1831.

school. Having one type of Sunday school hymns and then ex-
pecting the children to enjoy and appreciate the hymns announced in church worship is an exercise in futility. We will
again be training a generation of Christians who will always
find worship somewhat frustrating. Their complaint will be that
of their parents, "Why can't we sing something we know?"

What hymns should be sung? The church school planning
group should make sure that its students learn a central nucleus
of great hymns. Public school educators do not leave to chance
the introduction of excellent poetry and drama. Likewise a
church committee could study the official hymnal and decide
what hymns should be introduced in the various grades of the
school. Some hymnals (*The Church Hymnary, Third Edition,* for
example) have an asterisk beside those hymns in the First Lines
Index which are suited especially to children. Also use the list of
ecumenical hymns in Chapter 5 as a guide in your selection
process. Eskew and McElrath in *Sing with Understanding*[2] have
a high quality selection of 100 hymns for church school divided
into three age groupings. Of special note in their list are the
asterisks which indicate those hymns for which the Choristers
Guild has prepared study sheets. For information regarding the
Guild, see page 4.

Two Practical Suggestions

1. *Ask the musicians to help.*   Most staff musicians are re-
ally church music educators who are concerned with leading the
members into fuller Christian knowledge and experience. The
organist/choirmaster plus certain singers in the adult and youth
choirs could be made available to assist teachers in the utilization of hymns in the lesson plans. If it is not a regular custom,
try to arrange occasions when a number of classes can assemble
for worship and for the enjoyment of singing a number of hymns.

2. *Use the Boyter method of teaching hymns.*   In an effort to
improve the quality of their congregational singing and to in-
sure its future, Mabel and Haskel Boyter of Atlanta, Georgia
developed a unique approach. In addition to urging and instruct-
ing the adults to participate in singing familiar and new hymns,

the Boyters attacked the problem from the 7-year old children up through the youth choirs.

In choir rehearsals, twenty-five new hymns were taught the children during the season (October to June.) In addition to this group work, a hymn memorizing contest was announced. It would extend from October 15 to May 15. The rules were as follows:

Each child was to
   a. memorize the melody,
   b. memorize the first stanza, and
   c. sing melody and first stanza from memory unaccompanied before the "listening committee."

Adequate records were kept and tabulated by a Hymn Chairman with monthly announcements of who was ahead in the contest. Such remarkable response was received that the listening committee had to be doubled within eight weeks' time.

The important feature regarding this project was the fact that these hymns were *selected and taught by the parents of the choristers*. This was the first wedge in a *family* project. Later, when enthusiasm was rampant, a "Family Hymn Sing" was announced, with recognition to be given the 100 percent families who were present. There were 23 families who were 100 percent present! Between 250 and 300 people attended and sang more enthusiastically than most of the Sunday morning congregations. The Hymn Sing was held Sunday afternoon between 3:30 and 4:30 o'clock. The fact that this "Sing" was announced as lasting exactly one hour played a large part in its success. All the promotional communications stated that even if the congregation was in the middle of a hymn, they could count on exactly one hour for this project. Besides improving congregational singing, it was hoped that through this "family affair" the old custom of family singing in the homes could be revived, at least to a certain extent.

A second "Sing" was held a month later with almost 400 people present and 27 families were 100 percent there. A revealing fact was *the exposure to 19 new hymns* besides many old or familiar hymns which were sung during the two one-hour sessions. The boys and girls who already knew these new hymns were urged to *hold hymnals with their fathers and mothers* and thus to lead them in the learning of new materials. At the same time a feeling of family togetherness was felt more and more strongly.

There were 972 hymns sung from memory by the 7-13 year olds in the two choirs from October 15 to May 15. The next year almost 1,300 hymns were sung. This wide experience with one stanza memorized was more valuable, it was felt, than many stanzas of fewer hymns. After all, the ages represented could read any number of stanzas, once they were acquainted with the hymn tune.

The follow-up of this project was the further extension into the church school and eventually into the congregational singing. With a nucleus of approximately 400 persons who had attended the Family Hymn-Sings, the enthusiasm for hymns was spread by these "torch bearers."

The minister of music, the director of Christian education, and a council from the departments of the church school chose the hymns to be sung in a church-wide hymn festival in the spring. These were sung throughout the year in the classes and then, when festival time came, *the church school sponsored it* as a part of the Christian education program and the music department assisted! This again increased the cooperation and fusion of the two departments.

The contest was extended to the playing of hymns also—on any instrument chosen. Mrs. Boyter explains: "In this way we hoped to grow our own Sunday school pianists and instrumentalists in time. Seventy-five percent of my junior choir members were studying privately, so why not capitalize on this! Some of them were going to make splendid pianists and soloists. The winner in this area of the contest played 108 hymns on the clarinet and a large number on piano also."

When five or ten minutes were available in some rehearsals, and opportunity was given for children to choose what they would sing, almost invariably hymns which they had learned during the year were requested.

Besides encouraging the learning of hymn tunes and words, Mrs. Boyter taught the singers to classify hymns by pattern or form. "As we learned hymns, we listed them under their own pattern and eventually we had quite a repertoire of hymns of different patterns. First we did this by colors. For instance, in singing "Joyful, joyful, we adore thee." we had red, yellow, green and blue strips of construction paper from which to choose.

"After the choir sang the first line of this hymn, we decided to call this theme red. Then the second line was sung and the question asked whether it was the same or different. The choir said, 'Same.' OK, pick up another red strip.

"This is the third line. Is it same or different?" 'Different.' "OK. pick up another color.

"This is the fourth line. Is it the same or different?

"'It is the same as one and two.' "OK. What do we have, class? 'Red, red, yellow, red.' "The children *loved* this."

For another approach to teaching hymns in the early years, be sure to read David Ng and Virginia Thomas *Children in the Worshipping Community*, (Paperback, John Knox Press, 1981), especially Chapter 7 "Leading Children into Worship through Music."

Perhaps a note of explanation should be added here about the wisdom of teaching the classic hymns to young children. The Scottish theologian, Donald Baillie, describes the value in these words:

> I once heard a wise man say that the best reason for learning by heart, in one's youth, great passages of poetry is because the poetry will then have deeper and deeper meanings put into it by the experience of life as the years go by. When you first learn it, you are young and immature, and it does not mean a great deal to you. But there it is, stored up in your mind; and as you go through life things happen, and experience grows, and the old bit of poetry comes home to you in new ways. You find in it something that you never suspected, new and richer meanings that perhaps even go beyond what the poet himself could have consciously thought or meant. How very true that is![3]

John Wesley expressed this same idea in the 1790 edition of his brother Charles' book of children's hymns:

> There are two ways of writing or speaking to children; the one is, to stoop down to them; the other, to lift them up to us. Dr. Watts wrote in the former way, and has succeeded admirably, speaking to children as children, and leaving them as he found them. The following

3. From *To Whom Shall We Go?* p. 137. Copyright © 1955 by John Baillie. Reprinted with the permission of The Saint Andrew Press, 121 George Street, Edinburgh.

hymns are written on the other plan: they contain strong imagery yet expressed in such plain and easy language that even children can understand. But when they do understand them, they will be children no longer, only in years and stature.[4]

Each church educational system is unique in some respects. Therefore study it and devise a hymn curriculum that suits the needs of your people, children and adults. The rewards will be limitless.

4. Quoted in Erik Routley's Article 16 "Hymns for Children, 1715-1900," p. 123 of *A Panorama of Christian Hymnody*. Dr. Routley has two other articles on children's hymns in this volume.

Chapter XIV

CONGREGATIONAL REHEARSALS

"For congregational singing to become the fine thing it may be, congregational practices are indispensable."[1] This observation by Sir Walford Davies and Dr. Harvey Grace contains the basic ingredient in a program to improve congregational singing.

If it is necessary for the minister, organist, choirmaster, and choir to spend time each week to perfect their part in public worship, it is indeed appropriate that occasionally—perhaps once a month—the congregation also have opportunity to practice its part in the worship of God through music.

If the title "Congregational Rehearsal" or "Congregational Practice" sounds forbidding and unattractive, call the event a "Hymn Sing" or even an "Old Fashioned Hymn Sing," "Exploring the Hymnal," or something else. The goal is to teach the entire congregation to enjoy singing a sizable number of good hymns with spiritual perception and musical artistry.

Herbert Wiseman had conducted many congregational practices in Scottish churches and had introduced fine but unfamiliar hymns in their *Revised Church Hymnary*. He remarked, "The congregations varied in composition, but in most cases they have been alike in showing an attitude of doubt at the beginning and of enthusiasm at the end of the practice."[2] This has been my

---

1. *Music & Worship,* p. 145. New York: H. W. Gray Company, 1935. Reprinted by AMS Press, New York.
2. *Manual of Church Praise according to the Use of the Church of Scotland.* Edinburgh: The Church of Scotland Committee on Publications, 1932. p. 150. Used by permission of The Saint Andrews Press, 121 George Street, Edinburgh.

experience without fail. Try a practice with the entire congregation if possible or with any segment which is available.

Time for Rehearsals

The Lutherans have two suggestions: "(1) Use the first 10 minutes of the service for several weeks—or begin the rehearsal 5 minutes before the service hour and go into the hour 5 more minutes. Find ways to shorten the rest of the service so they still get out on time if this is a touchy thing in your parish. Otherwise some negative feelings may result. (2) Use the announcement period for several weeks, cutting notices to a bare minimum."[3] I used the pre-service time once a month for years in a parish I served. In yet another parish we regularly employed twenty minutes of the weekly church night supper for singing hymns and basic hymnic instruction.

The Leader of Rehearsals

Remember that the people have assembled to sing hymns, not to listen to a lecture on the history of hymnody or voice production. Plan every moment of the practice and write down the lesson plan. Begin and end with a familiar hymn. Keep your comments and instructions succinct. I suggest that you write them down, memorize them, and keep your notes handy. "Writing maketh an exact man," Sir Francis Bacon said. Balance the learning of new hymns with gaining fresh insights into familiar ones. Look up the background of the hymns and give some of this information to your people.

The leader of this practice can be the minister, the choirmaster, or any member of the congregation. Anyone with a gift of informal leadership, a singing voice, and knowledge and love of good hymns could do it. The leader should stand in full view of the people and occasionally might rove up and down the aisles. The conductor's voice is a better teaching medium than playing the tune on the organ. Train your choirs (adult and/or children) in the hymns and use them to help teach. Simple gestures to

---

3. From *Guide to Introducing Lutheran Book of Worship.* (Copyright © 1973 by Augsburg Publishing House. Used by permission.)

outline the melody and give the beat are helpful. If you wish, use the standard conducting patterns described in Chapter 9. Sir Walford Davies suggests that "the less formal and schoolmasterish or ecclesiastical his method, the better."[4] Have your people sit most of the time but occasional standing for a hymn is welcome.

Enjoy yourself. Your enthusiasm will be contagious. Compliment and encourage the people on every progressive step. Keep in mind some of the basic laws of learning:

Readiness: create in your people an interest in their own music—hymns—so that they will be ready and eager to learn.

Gradualness: remember to grade your instruction and material so that you make steady progress toward the goal of great congregational singing. Do not tackle the toughest music in the hymnal at the first practice.

Repetition: remember that even the finest symphony orchestras need to repeat their music many times in the learning process. When you have introduced a new hymn, repeat it until it is fixed in the memories and affections of your congregation.

Here are some specific projects or themes for these practices. There are many others which your ingenuity will suggest.

1. *Introduce John Wesley's Directions for Singing.* Distribute sheets containing these rules.[5] Discuss them and illustrate each by singing hymns.

2. *Explain the items on a hymnal page.*[6] Show where the author's and composer's name and dates are located. Indicate the tune names and explain why some were given these particular names. McCutchan's *Hymn Tune Names* (Abingdon Press, 1957) and hymnal handbooks give these origins. Of interest to most groups is the indication of the poetic meter. Tell them that Long Meter (LM) 88.88 means eight syllables in each of the four lines of the stanza. Then have them sing the Doxology "Praise God

---

4. *Music & Worship,* p. 147.
5. These sheets can be purchased in quantities from Outlook Publishers, 512 East Main Street, Richmond, VA 23219. These Directions are listed in Chapter 2 of this book.
6. The formats of hymnal pages and hymn metrical patterns are discussed in Chapter 6.

from whom all blessings flow." Now show them the list of Long
Meter tunes in the Metrical Index. *Duke Street* would undoubtedly be one of them. Let the congregation sing the Doxology text
"Praise God from whom all blessing flow" to *Duke Street* (to
which "Jesus shall reign" is usually sung.)

Then explain Common and Short Meter and illustrate. If there
is time and interest, you might intimate what the rest of the
Metrical Index denotes with its serially rising numbers. The
group might be interested in looking at the 87.87.D section
where the tune for "What a friend we have in Jesus" *Converse* is
located along with *Ebenezer,* the tune for "Once to every man
and nation." The Scottish *Revised Church Hymnary* (1927) gives
the former words with the latter tune!

3. *Spend the time singing alternate tunes.* Explain why
some texts have two or more musical settings and sing each.
Here are a few samples which are given in many hymnals:

"Jesus, lover of my soul" *Martyn* and *Aberystwyth*
"Come, thou long expected Jesus" *Hyfrydol* and *Stuttgart*
"When I survey the wondrous cross" *Hamburg* and *Rocking-
ham Old*
"For all the saints" *Sine Nomine* and *Sarum*

4. *Explain the structure of hymn melodies.* Play over or
sing a folk tune like *Forest Green* which accompanies several
texts in most hymnals. Ask the people to tell you what sections
of the music were the same. They will probably have noted that
the first, second, and last lines were identical. You could indicate this on a blackboard by the formula AABA. Turn to several
other hymn tunes with this form. Mention and show that many
German chorales like *Lobe Den Herren* "Praise ye the Lord, the
Almighty, the King of Creation" and *Ein Feste Burg* "A mighty
Fortress is our God" repeat the same theme on the first two
lines.

The Welsh tune *Aberystwyth* has some interesting aspects.
Play the first two measures for the congregation. Tell them that
this theme is repeated three times in the whole tune. Play the
entire hymn and ask them where this phrase recurs. You might
also use the third line to explain what a musical sequence is—a
brief snatch of melody or a phrase which is repeated immediately at a higher or lower pitch. The melody of "Fairest

Lord Jesus" has two sets of sequences. Your group might be fascinated by the economy of structure in *Lasst Uns Erfreuen* "All creatures of our God and King." The pattern is AABBCCBBBBB.

The amount of direct imitation (repetition of a phrase on the same pitch) and sequence in "Silent night" is astounding. The first four-note phrase is repeated four times! But there are hymn tunes like *Slane* "Be Thou my vision" and *Sine Nomine* "For all the saints" which possess beautiful musical rhetoric without much obvious thematic repetition.

5. *Teach a new hymn by rote.* Assuming you do not have many music readers in your group, try Sir Walford Davies' method. It works. I've tried it.

> A congregation of good average intelligence and musical ability . . . can soon read a new tune after it is sung or played once. If the conditions are less favorable, a line at a time is a good method. Words and music alike are more thoroughly taught, and the singers kept on the alert, by some such plan as this (with a four-line hymn):
> First line of verse 1 [the British call a stanza a verse.]
> First line of verse 2
> Second line of verse 2
> First two lines of verse 3
> Third line of verse 1
> Fourth line of verse 2
> The whole of verse 4
> This may appear to be fussy, but it works, because it spreads the study beyond the first verse; the repetition of the musical phrase to a fresh verbal phrase is good memory-training; and, above all, it keeps the interest alive.[7]

If you plan to teach *Bryn Calfaria,* which Erik Routley calls a "piece of real Celtic rock,"[8] anchor the first two lines which are identical. The melody of these lines rises like a vigorous hike up a Welsh mountainside. The third line is a series of three rising sequences. The final line begins with three rapidly cascading sequences. This is the only real tricky spot. Have your group sing this last line first using *ta-ta-ta,* then words. It goes without saying that before you teach any new tunes you should know them "cold."

6. *Concentrate one practice on the texts of hymns.* Since we know that almost everyone can read English, we assume they

---

7. *Music & Worship*, p. 148.
8. *Companion to Congregational Praise*, p. 84. London: Independent Press, Ltd., 1953.

automatically understand what the hymn text is about. John
Wesley knew that this was not necessarily so. He wrote, "Have
an eye to God in every word you sing... In order to do this
attend strictly to the sense of what you sing, and see that your
heart is not carried away with the sound..."[9]

To enable your people to follow this advice, suggest that they
make a habit of reading the texts of the service hymns during
the few moments before public worship begins. Suggest that
they make a mental note to whom each hymn is addressed. For
examples, "Holy, Holy, Holy, Lord God Almighty" is addressed
to God; Jesus Christ is the One to whom we speak in "Fairest
Lord Jesus," and in "Fight the good fight" we are exhorting our
neighbor. In "Bless, O my soul, the living Lord" we are talking to
ourselves.

Explaining how certain hymns came to be written helps folk
to understand many texts.

Select a hymn like "Where cross the crowded ways of life" and
point out the many explicit references to biblical passages. Explain that Christian theology is expressed concisely in many
hymns. Three stanzas of "Ancient of Days" are devoted to explaining the Three Persons of the Trinity.

7. *Explain and utilize many alternate ways of singing.* Antiphonal (between two groups of singers) and responsorial (between a soloist and a group) singing are two obvious and ancient
means of variation. Women and men, two sides of the church,
choir versus congregation, soloist and congregation—the possibilities are numerous. Try "Watchman, tell us of the night"
with a soloist as the watchman and the congregation as the
travelers. The tune *Lasst Uns Erfreuen* can be exciting with two
sides of the congregation answering alternate phrases with all
joining together in the last Alleluia. Incidentally the usual
Doxology text "Praise God from whom all blessings flow" becomes festive when sung to *Lasst Uns Erfreuen*—interspersing
Alleluias on theme B.

Here are some other variation resources which should be explained and demonstrated: descants, melody in tenor, unison
singing, unaccompanied singing, alternate harmonization. Concerning this last item, be sure to instruct the congregation to
shift to the melody when a free or varied accompaniment is

9. See footnote No. 5 above.

played on the organ, otherwise the habitual altos and basses will be puzzled and perhaps outraged at being deprived of their accustomed part.

8. *Teach the congregation short responses, versicles, and canticles.* Many denominations expect the congregations to join in musical expressions other than hymns. A congregational practice is an ideal time to teach them. Those denominations which include these non-hymnic materials usually provide instructional materials and recordings to assist in congregational tuition. The Lutherans, for example, have a section on how to teach the three musical settings of the Holy Communion and the chanting of the Psalms in their *Guide to Introducing Lutheran Book of Worship* (Augsburg Publishing House, 1978.)

9. *Teach your congregation some rudiments of music.* How does one go about teaching a congregation to read music? Certainly an urban congregation cannot be expected to attend a singing school for as long as our forebears did. Many of us have seen the lengthy musical catechisms which are at the beginning of early American tunebooks like William Walker's *Southern Harmony* (1835) and B. F. White and E. J. King's *Sacred Harp* (1844). These texts enabled many of our ancestors to read music. Even if we cannot spend this amount of time and effort, we can move our congregations closer to music literacy. The degree of progress will depend in part on the leader's knowledge and skill and partly on the amount of time which can be devoted by the congregation to this project.

The problem of congregational music literacy has engaged the attention of many innovators. In England, John Curwen (1816–1880) developed and promoted the Tonic Sol-Fa system. As a result, there are hymnals with the following symbols which indicate the pitches and time values of the four hymn parts. Here is the first line of the Welsh tune *Bryn Calfaria* in Tonic Sol-Fa notation. It comes from a Welsh hymn book:

Another method of indicating the music of hymns is the use of shape notes placed on the five staff lines. The Mennonites (1969) and the Southern Baptists (1975) have published shape-note versions of their newest hymnals. Here is *Bryn Calfaria* in shape notation:

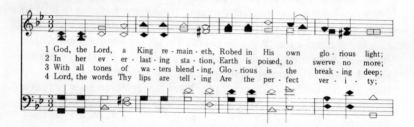

1 God, the Lord, a King re - main - eth, Robed in His own glo - rious light;
2 In her ev - er - last - ing sta - tion, Earth is poised, to swerve no more;
3 With all tones of wa - ters blend - ing, Glo - rious is the break - ing deep;
4 Lord, the words Thy lips are tell - ing Are the per - fect ver - i - ty;

Most denominational hymnals, however, have staff notation and this is what congregational leaders need to teach their congregations. There may be at least three reactions to this statement. First, there may be readers who for a variety of reasons can make no attempt to teach music reading to their congregation. These persons might make some use of rote learning earlier described in Section 5. Second, there are leaders who could give a few elemental instructions and hints about music notation in a congregational rehearsal. Third, there may be some leaders and congregations able to work enthusiastically toward helping a congregation to read hymns—both text *and tune.*

The scope of this chapter precludes the exposition of a course in music reading. Fortunately there is an excellent and inexpensive text which will give you a skillful way to teach staff notation to your congregation. Be sure to purchase and study Howard Shanet's *Learn to Read Music* (Simon and Schuster, revised paperback edition.) It is thorough and slanted to teaching large groups. Shanet has taught thousands to read music in four hours of class work using his method and exercises. Obviously, application of his methods can be divided into smaller time units and the content adapted for your group.

The Notation of Rhythm

Give your congregation instructions like the following statements which are abbreviations of Shanet's text.[10]

10. Copyright © 1956 by Howard Shanet. Reprinted by permission of Simon & Schuster, a Division of Gulf & Western Corporation.

With the toe of your foot, tap steadily four beats or pulses at about the speed of a military march, over and over again and count aloud, accenting the *one* count:

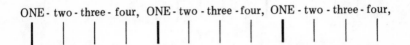

ONE - two - three - four, ONE - two - three - four, ONE - two - three - four,

Now sing one long *Ta* on any comfortable pitch and make it one long sound while you continue to tap with your toe, accenting the *one* beat.

Sing: Ta

Tap:

ONE 2 3 4 ONE 2 3 4 ONE 2 3 4

Now let's try tones of different lengths. In the following exercise, continue tapping but hold each tone only as long as the line after it indicates.

Sing: Ta   Ta   Ta   Ta

Tap:

Do the same with the following exercise which involves shorter tones, each syllable being held for only two beats:

Sing: Ta__ Ta__ Ta__ Ta__ Ta__ Ta__ Ta__ Ta__

Tap:

Now we combine these two types:

Sing: Ta__ Ta__ Ta   Ta__ Ta__ Ta

Tap:

Here is a third kind, in which each tone is held for the length

of one single beat or tap. We combine it immediately with one of
the longer types, just for the sake of variety:

Then you could explain that the four-beat tone is indicated by
a whole note, the two-beat tone by a half note, and the one beat
by the quarter note. Show the group what these notes look like.
Then you could show the following chart or use the hymnbook
notation of this hymn:

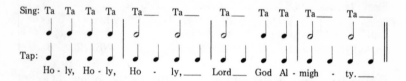

Shanet begins his rhythm instructions with exercises and
comments like the above illustrations. Obviously there are
many details of time notation which have been omitted here
(smaller fraction notes, time signatures, dotted and tied notes,
etc.) but maybe the congregation's appetite for further literacy
skills has been whetted.

Words Copyright © 1982 in HYMNS AND THEIR USES by Agape.
International Copyright Secured. All Rights Reserved.
Tune from "The Ditty Bag" compiled by Janet Tobitt.
Published by Girl Scouts of the U.S.A.

This Danish three-part round is an excellent and fun way to teach a congregation various note lengths. Clocks of three sizes strike at different speeds represented by note values of three lengths. If you wished to put it on a blackboard, you could double the time values of each note if you wished to show different notation lengths. Sung in three parts, this round gives a fascinating and beautiful effect.

The Notation of Pitch

You could draw eight ascending lines on the blackboard and number each 1 through 8 starting at the bottom. Explain that melodies are based on a musical ladder called a scale. Sing the scale using these numbers and have the people join you. Then sing the first phrase of the melody of "Holy, Holy, Holy, Lord God Almighty" using the numbers 1-1-3-3-5-5-6-6-6-5-3, pointing to the numbered lines on the blackboard as you sing. Do the same with other familiar tunes like *Hymn To Joy, Ein Feste Burg,* and *Antioch.* Now draw a C major scale on the five line staff and do the same tunes the same way in this key pointing to notes as they go up and down.

Then have the congregation turn in their hymnals to a familiar hymn in C major and show them that the melody lies in the top line of notes. Believe it or not, many persons have no notion that the melody is indicated by the contour of the separate dots at the top of the music. Do not worry yourself and the congregation at this stage with the distinction between whole and half steps, intervals, sharps and flats, key signatures, diatonic and chromatic scales, etc. This could come later, if not to the entire congregation, then to a smaller group interested in additional instruction. At least, the congregation can be urged to watch the melody line of notes whenever a hymn is played because that is where the tune is located.

In all these efforts to teach music notation, keep in mind that your congregation is not unmusical but that the majority probably cannot read staff notation. The average pew occupant can read the English text aloud with no hesitation or embarrassment. But ask these same persons to attach these words to an unfamiliar tune and they will balk. Why? Most of them simply do not know how to translate audibly those dots, vertical bars, accidentals, time signatures, etc., into a melody.

Of course, you may have a number of persons who are good readers of music notation. They are apt to be located, incidentally, in the choir. And there are exceptional congregations, like that student body of a choir college, which can tackle successfully any music in the hymnal.

Herbert Wiseman expressed this writer's opinion exactly when he wrote, "Congregations through the land are willing and eager to learn. They are looking for guidance. If our organists will take up this subject seriously, and realize that it requires a technique of its own just as much as organ playing does, there is no reason why. congregational singing, in even the smallest churches, should not become a worthy and acceptable offering."[11]

---

11. *Manual of Church Praise according to the Use of the Church of Scotland,* 157.

Chapter XVI

ACOUSTICS AND THEIR EFFECT ON CONGREGATIONAL SINGING

The magnificent tone of a Stradivarius violin depends in large measure upon cavity resonance. This means that the vibrations, which leave the strings as the bow activates them, pass into the marvelously shaped interior of the violin. Here the sound waves are selectively modified and amplified so that the tones which emerge and reach the ears of the audience are considered magnificent. A Stradivarius stuffed with cotton would trap these vibrations and seriously and adversely affect the tone of the instrument.

In like manner the cavity of an auditorium, surrounded by the floor, walls, and ceiling, acts upon a tone generated within its confines. The tone of voices, a piano, an organ will either be deadened or will be glorified by the acoustical environment. Consequently it is of enormous importance to a congregation to see that optimum acoustical conditions prevail in the church sanctuary.

A certain generous member of the congregation, who enjoys wall-to-wall carpeting, draperies, and overstuffed furniture at home, might donate a lovely deep red carpet for the entire church floor. Unfortunately this act of philanthropy may well take the keen edge off congregational singing for the duration of the life of the rug. In fact, I know of a church interior which not only has wall-to-wall carpeting, pew cushions, but also absorptive fabric attached to front and back of each pew back. Needless to say, the acoustics are atrocious. A hard, reflective, waxed cork or rubber tile flooring could conceivably make as splendid a gift and yet retain acoustical vibrancy for the interior.

Sir James Jeans, celebrated British physicist, speaking of this acoustical phenomenon, says that sufficient reverberation in an auditorium "... naturally induces an exhilarating feeling of effortless power." Of a non-reverberant room, he further says that this "produces the despair of ineffectual struggle."[1]

Another authority, James Blanton, writes:

> The current extensive and indiscriminate use of sound-absorbing materials in churches is one of the most deplorable developments in contemporary church practice. It is a common experience today for a church group to spend several thousand dollars for sound-absorbing materials which render the interior of their new church acoustically dead. This in turn calls for the spending of hundreds of dollars more for an amplifying system to enable the congregation to hear the preacher and many more thousands of dollars for additional ranks of pipes for the organ which would be wholly unnecessary if they had not spent the money for the acoustical materials in the first place. This is a vicious sequence of expenditures which ends up with the church having put out a lot of extra money for an inferior result; in some cases of very large projects these ill-advised expenditures reach prodigious sums.[2]

What happens specifically when vibrations leave the throats of the congregation and minister or the organ pipes? These sound waves pass through the air until they hit a surface. Here they are either reflected to some other surface or they are absorbed. Everyone has seen the little holes in acoustical blocks. The vibrations pass into these holes and are trapped. Most of the sound does not emerge. The same thing happens when vibrations hit clothing, draperies, pew cushions, and non-acoustical carpeting.

In public dining rooms, in halls of school buildings and in all places where much noise is generated and little sound is wanted—these are places where sound damping is indicated.

The difference between acoustical reverberation and echo should be made clear. An echo in a church is objectionable. It could cause a confusing repetition of the minister's words or a jumble of the music. This phenomenon can be controlled by care-

1. *Science & Music*, p. 212. Cambridge: Cambridge University Press, 1937.
2. From *The Organ in Church Design*, p. 111. Albany, TX: Venture Press, 1957.
   (Copyright © 1957 by Joseph E. Blanton. Used by permission.)

fully planning the shape of the building interior and in some cases by the careful application of absorbent materials. On the other hand, adequate reverberation permits not only the audition of the initial line-of-sight sound but also the many additional reflections of vibrations which give strength and richness to the original sound.

At a rehearsal I have stood in the chancel of some churches and heard the complete tonal spectrum of a great organ and choir, but as I walked halfway down the aisle, the tone progressively deteriorated. What had happened was that the beautiful initial tones were being swallowed up in the millions of traps in the cinderblock walls of the chancel and auditorium, or in the myriad recesses of pew cushions, or in the deep piling of the carpets, or in the 2,348,971 holes in the ceiling blocks.

In planning for a new church sanctuary, be sure to engage an architect who has a track record of planning acoustically excellent church interiors. If the present worship room has inferior acoustics, keep in mind that corrective measures are possible. The acoustical blocks can be painted over to obliterate the absorption pores. The carpets can be replaced with hard tile or other flooring. If carpets are mandatory, select the sort which are made of the new acoustically efficient material which absorbs very little of the vibrations.

During a service in a church with good acoustics, the worshippers, when singing, can hear each other and are mutually encouraged. They realize more completely that they are part of the community of believers.

The interior of a church is an instrument—an instrument of God—and it should be so formed that His praise, whether vocal or instrumental, is beautiful and full of meaning.

Chapter XVII

HYMN FESTIVALS AND SERVICES

A hymn festival is a celebration of the Christian faith through congregational song. Each year thousands of Christians in scores of communities throughout the country and the world join in hymn festivals.[1] These inspiring services, whether denominational or interdenominational, have been sponsored by groups such as rural or urban ministerial association, an organists' guild chapter, a music club, a council of churches, or the Hymn Society of America. They may celebrate a festival like Reformation Sunday, one of the major festivals of the church year, the culmination of a great convention or conference, or other occasions.

Under expert leadership and surrounded by throngs of singing Christians, a layperson usually gains a completely new experience of praise through song. This person takes back to the local congregation a new concept of stimulating, intelligent singing. The seeds of positive influence planted by such festivals are numberless. Of course, local leaders do not have to wait for a large cooperative hymn festival to be planned. They can organize a service based on hymns for their own members and can utilize the ideas in this chapter in planning this service.

In a specific order for a hymn service or festival, it is probably wise to begin and end with a familiar hymn. In fact the majority of the hymns perhaps ought to be at least moderately familiar to most of the group. Each detail of the service be meticulously planned. The leader should be capable, well prepared and en-

---

1. These festivals are listed from time to time in *The Stanza* which is the newsletter of the Hymn Society of America.

thusiastic. Vigorous hymns should be alternated with quieter ones for a change of mood. The singing can be varied by the use of descants, melody-in-the-tenor arrangements, varied harmonic accompaniments, and hymn anthems. A variety of instrumental accompaniments add interest. Alternation of stanzas between the various vocal forces (two sides of the congregation, men and women, congregation and choir, soloist and congregation) can be employed. Stories of several of the hymns might be helpful. All comments, however, should be brief, clear, and interesting. Omit certain stanzas upon occasion if desired and perhaps have the congregation read some of the stanzas. For part of the festival it might be helpful to have the choir members move out of the chancel or choir loft and mingle with the congregation in order, by their proximity, to give new courage and enthusiasm to the laypersons.

Several Examples of Hymn Festivals

1. When the United Nations was formally organized in San Francisco in 1946, the Richmond, Virginia chapter of the American Guild of Organists and the local ministerial association joined in sponsoring a large hymn festival to celebrate the occasion. Because of the great interest manifested, it was decided to engage the largest civic auditorium available (3667 capacity.) Forty-seven vested choirs with more than a thousand singers were placed in groups of about sixty persons here and there in the vast packed congregation. Clergymen from four different denominations participated in the leadership.

The theme of this festival was "One World in Christ." The processional hymn was "In Christ there is no east or west." Hymns from many different nations were sung after a brief spoken comment by the leader. For example, "A mighty Fortress is our God" represented Germany. Its first two stanzas were sung by congregation and choirs in the key of C. Only the choirs unaccompanied sang the third stanza. Then the organ and brass modulated to the key of D and, with all the choristers singing the melody in unison with the congregation, the hymn concluded in a brilliant way. The brief (10 minutes) sermon had as its topic "Once to every man and nation" as the worshippers considered the momentous inauguration of the United Nations that very day.

Since it was impossible to assemble enough hymnals for this throng, the festival organizers printed a special sixteen-page booklet which contained not only the order of service with the text and music of the hymns but also John Wesley's Directions for Singing.

2. The following order of worship for a festival of hymns based on the life of Christ was originally developed by the Rev. George L. Knight. The hymnals cited in this order are the Lutheran *Service Book and Hymnal* (1958) and the Lutheran *Worship Supplement* (St. Louis: Concordia Publishing House.)

ONE WORLD IN CHRIST

Prelude: Improvisation on "King's Weston"   Worship Supplement 743
Hymn: *At The Name Of Jesus*   Arr. D. Busarow

1. All (seated)	5. All
2. Choir	6. Choir
3. Women	7. All
4. Men	(standing)

I. BIRTH

Hymn: *O Sing A Song Of Bethlehem*   (Kingsfold)
         (standing)

O sing a song of Bethlehem, Of shepherds watching there,
And of the news that came to them From angels in the air:
The light that shone on Bethlehem Fills all the world today;
Of Jesus' birth and peace on earth The angels sing alway.

Reading: Matthew 1:18–25
Hymns: *Of The Father's Love Begotten*   Service Book and
                                 Hymnal No. 17

1. All (seated)	4. All	(1st setting)
2. Women	5. All	
3. Men	(standing)	

From Heav'n Above To Earth I Come   No. 22, SBH

All five stanzas sung in parts,
unaccompanied

NB "Amen" will be sung where printed.

II. BOYHOOD

Hymn: (Kingsfold)

O sing a song of Nazareth, Of sunny days of joy;
O sing of fragrant flowers' breath, And of the sinless boy:
For now the flowers of Nazareth In ev'ry heart may grow;
Now spreads the fame of his dear name On all the winds that blow.

Reading: Luke 2:41-52
Hymns: *Our Father, By Whose Name*   Worship Supplement 782
                                                 Arr. D. Busarow
                1. Choir   3. All
                2. Choir

                Within Thy Father's House   (St. Michael)

1. (all)   Within the Father's house The Son hath found his home,
                And to his temple suddenly The Lord of Life hath come.
2. (men)   The doctors of the Law Gaze on the wondrous Child
                And marvel at his gracious words Of wisdom undefiled,
3. (women)   Yet not to them is giv'n The mighty truth to know,
                To lift the earthly veil which hides Incarnate God below.
4. (all)   The secret of the Lord Escapes each human eye,
                And faithful pondering hearts await The full epiphany.

Verses 5, 6, and 7 spoken in prayer:
                Lord, visit Thou our souls And teach us by Thy grace
                Each dim revealing of Thyself With loving awe to trace,
                Till from our darkened sight The cloud shall pass away
                And on the cleansed soul shall burst The everlasting day,
                Till we behold Thy face And know as we are known
                Thee, Father, Son, and Holy Ghost, Coequal Three in One.
                                                          AMEN

III. LIFE AND MINISTRY

Hymn: (Kingfold)

O sing a song of Galilee, Of lake and woods and hill,
Of him who walked upon the sea And bade its waves be still:
For though, like waves of Galilee, Dark seas of trouble roll,
When faith has heard the Master's word, Falls peace upon the soul.

Reading: Matthew 8:5-13
Hymns: *Songs Of Thankfulness And Praise*   No. 55, SBH
                Everyone sings all stanzas   (St. George's Windsor)

                The King Of Love My Shepherd Is   No. 530, SBH
                                                           (St. Columba)

                1. All   4. Men
                2. Women   5. Canon
                3. Canon   (men—
                   (women   women)
                   begin—men   6. All
                   follow one
                   measure
                   later)

IV. SUFFERING AND DEATH

Hymn: (Kingfold)

O sing a song of Calvary, Its glory and dismay;
Of him who hung upon the tree, And took our sins away:

For he who died on Calvary Is risen from the grave,
And Christ, our Lord, by heav'n adored, Is mighty now to save.

Reading: Luke 23:26-49
Hymns: *O Sacred Head, Now Wounded*   No. 88, SBH
                                                                (2nd setting)
    1. All   3. All (unison)
    2. All   4. All
       (harmony   (harmony)
       without
       organ)

                Ah, Holy Jesus   No. 85, SBH

    1. All   3. Organ alone
    2. Canon (left   4. Canon (right
       side begins—   side—left
       right side   side)
       follows one   5. All
       measure
       later)

V.   RESURRECTION

Reading: Luke 24:1-12
Hymns: *Come, Ye Faithful, Raise The Strain*   Worship Supplement 738

                Everyone sings all stanzas,
                standing on verse 4

                Now Let The Vault of Heav'n   No. 103, SBH
                Resound

    1. All   3. Antiphonally
    2. Antiphonally   (women—
       by phrases   men)
       (') left side—   4. All
       right side,   (standing)
       all on final
       Alleluia

The Prayers:

Closing   *All Praise To Thee, My God, This*   No. 223, SBH
Hymn: *Night*

    1. All   3. Women
       (harmony)   4. Canon (left
    2. Canon (men   side—right
       begin—   side)
       women fol-   5. All (unison)
       low one
       measure
       later)

On September 9, 1979, a noteworthy hymn festival was held in Germany. Heinz Werner Zimmerman described it: "As far as I know, this 'Kirchenlieder-Festival' in Worms on the Rhine will be the first Hymn Festival in Germany . . . We'd like to show to the public the varied means church music has at its disposal, and to show the church musicians what to do with these means. We are deeply convinced that church music can be alive only as long as the church hymns are alive. For this reason we want to do something for them."[2]

Topics for Hymn Festivals

We do not have space to give detailed plans for each topic which we shall now suggest. These services can be planned by anyone who is imaginatively interested in hymnody. The various indexes of the hymnal (topical, authors and composers, scriptural allusions) will be of help in discovering appropriate hymns. Various handbooks suggested in the Bibliography will give background information for comments.

—*Hymns based on Psalm 23.* "The Lord's my Shepherd, I'll not want," "The King of Love my Shepherd is," "Saviour, like a Shepherd lead me," and "In heavenly love abiding" are based in varying degrees on the Shepherd Psalm.

—*God in nature.* "All creatures of our God and King," "Fairest Lord Jesus," "All beautiful the march of days," and "This is my Father's world" are but a few of dozens of hymns dealing with the world of nature. Projected slide pictures of beautiful natural scenes are sometimes shown to emphasize concepts and images in the hymn stanzas.

History of the Christian Church in hymns. Seven or eight of the significant eras of Christianity could be sketched and illustrated by appropriate hymns. The list of hymns in Chapter 5 could be of help in developing this type of service or festival.

—*Hymn tunes by great composers.* J. S. Bach, Ludwig van Beethoven, Joseph Haydn, and Ralph Vaughan Williams and many other composers are listed in the composers' index.

—*Hymn writers of various denominations.* Many separate

2. From *The Hymn* of The Hymn Society of America. October, 1979. p. 277. Used by permission.

branches of Christendom are represented in the hymnal. Among them are Presbyterian—Bonar and Matheson; Episcopal—Brooks and Heber; Methodist—the Wesleys and North; Baptist—Fawcett; Lutheran—Luther and Gerhardt.

—*Types of hymn tunes.* The list of types of hymn tunes with examples (see page 72) will help in shaping this service.

—*Welsh hymn festival.* The Welsh folk call this "Gymanfa Ganu" which literally means 'A Gathering for Song.' It could include such tunes as *Hyfrydol, Aberystwyth, Merionydd, Llanfair, Cwm Rhondda,* and *Ebenezer.*

Some of the following titles may suggest a fruitful topic for a hymn festival: Important Doctrines in Hymns; Metrical Psalms; Hymns by Jews, Protestants, and Roman Catholics; Hymn Writers in Various Professions; Dramatized Hymn Stories; Alternate Tunes to Well-Known Hymns; Hymns of Faith, Hope, and Love; Hymn of the Inner and Outer Life; and The Book of Revelation in Hymns.

Paper XXXI of The Hymn Society of America, titled *Hymn Festivals,* was written by Dr. Austin Lovelace. This valuable document includes a history of the hymn festival movement, the purpose and function of a festival, types, planning procedures, resources, and varied treatment of hymns. The paper concludes with some examples of service orders. It may be secured from the Society office, Wittenberg University, Springfield, Ohio 45501.

BIBLIOGRAPHY

Clark, Keith C. *A Selective Bibliography for the Study of Hymns 1980*. Paper XXXIII of The Hymn Society of America, Wittenberg University Springfield, Ohio 45501.

Companions/Handbooks to Hymnals

Dearmer, Percy, compiler. *Songs of Praise Discussed*. London: Oxford University Press, 1933.

Douglas, Charles Winfred; Ellinwood, Leonard; and others. *The Hymnal 1940 Companion*. New York: The Church Pension Fund, 1951.

Frost, Maurice. *Historical Companion to Hymns Ancient and Modern*. London: Wm. Clowes and Sons, Ltd., 1962.

*Gealy, Fred; Lovelace, A. C.; Young, Carlton R. *Companion to the Hymnal* (Methodist, 1964). Nashville: Abingdon Press, 1970.

Haeussler, Armin. *The Story of Our Hymns*. St. Louis: Eden Publishing House, 1952.

Hostetler, L., ed. *Handbook to the Mennonite Hymnary*. Newton, Kan.: 1949.

McCutchan, R. G. *Our Hymnody: A Manual of the Methodist Hymnal* (1935). Nashville: Abingdon Press, 1937.

Moffatt, James, and Patrick, Millar, editors. *Handbook to the Church Hymnary*. With supplement. London: Oxford University Press, 1935.

Osborne, Stanley L. *If Such Holy Song: The Story of the Hymns of The Hymn Book 1971*. Whitby, Ontario: The Institute of Church Music, 1976.

Parry, K. L. and Routley, Erik. *Companion to Congregational Praise*. London: The Independent Press, 1953.

Polack, William G. *The Handbook to the Lutheran Hymnal*. Reprint of 1958 third and revised edition. St. Louis: Concordia Publishing House, 1975.

Reynolds, William J. *Companion to Baptist Hymnal*. Nashville: Broadman Press, 1976.

*Ronander, Albert C., and Porter, Ethel K. *Guide to the Pilgrim Hymnal*. Philadelphia: United Church Press, 1966.

*Stulken, Marilyn Kay. *Hymnal Companion to the Lutheran Book of Worship*. Philadelphia: Fortress Press, 1981.

Concordances, Dictionaries, Indexes

Diehl, Katharine Smith. *Hymns and Tunes—an Index*. Metuchen, N.J.: Scarecrow Press, 1966.

Sadie, Stanley, editor. *The New Grove Dictionary of Music and Musicians*. 20 vols. London: Macmillan Publishers, Ltd. 1980.

Julian, John, editor. *A Dictionary of Hymnology*. A Reprint of the 1907 edition. 2 vols. New York: Dover Publications, 1957.

McDormand, Thomas B.; Crossman, Frederic S. *Judson Concordance to Hymns.* Valley Forge: The Judson Press, 1965.

*Schalk, Carl, editor. *Key Words in Church Music.* St. Louis: Concordia Publishing House, 1978.

Wackernagle, Philipp. *Das deutsche Kirchenlied vom der ältestan Zeit bis zu Anfang des XVIII Jahrhunderts.* 5 vols. Reprint of 1841 edition. Hildesheim: George Olms Verlagsbuchhandlung, 1964.

Zahn, Johannes. *Die Melodien der deutschen evangelischen Kirchenlieder.* 6. vols. Gütersloh: Bertelsmann, 1889-1893. Reprint ed. Hildesheim: George Olms, 1962.

The History and Practice of Hymns

Benson, Louis F. *The English Hymn: Its Development and Use in Worship.* New York: George H. Doran Co., 1915. Reprint, 1962, John Knox Press.

_____. *The Hymnody of the Christian Church.* Philadelphia: Westminster Press, 1927. Reprint, 1956, John Knox Press.

Blume, Friedrich, et. al. *Protestant Church Music: A History.* New York: W. W. Norton & Company, 1974.

Christ-Janer, Albert; Hughes, Charles W.; Smith, Carleton Sprague. *American Hymns Old and New.* New York: Columbia University Press, 1980.

_____. *The Companion Volume.* Historical and musical background information on each hymn in preceding volume. Same publisher.

Douglas, Winfred. *Church Music in History and Practice: Studies in the Praise of God.* New York: Charles Scribner's Songs, 1937. Revised edition by Leonard Ellinwood, 1962.

*Eskew, Harry; McElrath, Hugh T. *Sing with Understanding: An Introduction to Christian Hymnology.* Nashville: Broadman Press, 1980. This volume has an excellent and extensive bibliography.

Foote, H. W. *Three Centuries of American Hymnody.* Hamden, Conn.: Shoe String Press, 1961.

Frost, Maurice. *English and Scottish Psalm and Hymn Tunes.* London: Oxford University Press, 1953.

_____. *Historical Companion to Hymns Ancient and Modern.* London: Wm. Clowes and Sons, Ltd., 1962. Its 124 page introduction is a classic historical sketch of the development of hymnody.

*Halter, Carl; Schalk, Carl. *A Handbook of Church Music.* St. Louis: Concordia Publishing House, 1978.

Johnson, David. *Organ Teachers Guide.* Minneapolis: Augsburg Publishing House, 1971.

Leupold, Ulrich S., editor. *Liturgy and Hymns.* Volume 53 of *Luther's Works.* Philadelphia: Fortress Press, 1965.

*Lovelace, Austin; Rice, William. *Music and Worship in the Church,* Revised and Enlarged Edition. Nashville: Abingdon Press, 1976.

*Lovelace, Austin C. *The Anatomy of Hymnody.* Nashville: Abingdon Press, 1965.

*_____. *The Organist and Hymn Playing.* Revised. Carol Stream, Illinois: Agape, 1962, 1981.

McCutchan, R. G. *Hymn Tune Names.* Nashville: Abingdon Press, 1957.

Miller, L. David. *Hymns: The Story of Christian Song.* Philadelphia: Lutheran Church Press, 1969.

Moyer, J. Edward. *The Voice of His Praise: A New Appreciation of Hymnody.* Nashville: Graded Press, 1965.

Patrick, Millar. *Four Centuries of Scottish Psalmody.* London: Oxford University Press, 1949.

_____. *The Story of the Church's Song.* Edinburgh: Scottish Churches Joint Committee on Youth, 1927. Second edition revised for American Use by James R. Sydnor. 1962. John Knox Press.

Phillips, C. S. *Hymnody Past and Present*. London: SPCK, 1937.
Riedel, Johannes. *The Lutheran Chorale, Its Basic Traditions*. Minneapolis: Augsburg
    Publishing House, 1967.
Routley, Erik. *Hymns and Human Life*. New York: The Philosophical Library, 1952.
_____. *Hymns and the Faith*. London: Murray, 1955.
*_____. *Hymns Today and Tomorrow*. Nashville: Abingdon Press, 1964.
*_____. *An English-Speaking Hymnal Guide*. Collegeville: The Liturgical Press, 1979.
*_____. *A Panorama of Christian Hymnody*. Collegeville: The Liturgical Press, 1979.
_____. *I'll Praise My Maker*. London: Independent Press, 1951.
_____. *The Music of Christian Hymnody*. London: Independent Press, 1957.
_____. *The Music of Christian Hymns*. Chicago: G. I. A. Publications, Inc., 1981.
*_____. *Church Music and the Christian Faith*. Carol Stream, Illinois. Agape, 1978.
Ryden, E. E. *The Story of Christian Hymnody*. Rock Island, Ill.: Augustana Book Con-
    cern, 1959.
Thompson, Bard. *Liturgies of the Western Church*. Cleveland: The World Publishing
    Company, 1962.

Periodicals

Choristers Guild Letters. P.O. Box 38188, Dallas, TX 75238.
Church Music. 3558 South Jefferson Ave., St. Louis, MO 63118.
The Hymn. The Hymn Society of America, Wittenberg University, Springfield, Ohio
    45501.
Bulletin of The Hymn Society of Great Britain and Ireland. 30 East Meads, Guildford,
    Surrey GU2 5SP, England.
Journal of Church Music. Fortress Press, 2900 Queen Lane, Philadelphia, PN 19129.
Reformed Liturgy and Music. Joint Office of Worship, 1004 Alta Vista Road, Louisville,
    KY 40205.
Response. Valparaiso University, Valparaiso, Indiana.
Worship. Benedictines of St. John's Abbey, Collegeville, Minn.

Recent Hymnals

Break Not the Circle. 1975. Fred Kaan. Hope Publishing Company (Agape), No. 423.
Cantate Domino. Polyglot hymnal. 1974 edition. Bärenreiter BA 4994. (Organ edition,
    Oxford University Press.)
Ecumenical Praise. 1977. Hope Publishing Company (Agape), Carol Stream, Illinois
    60187.
English Praise. 1975. Oxford University Press.
Hymns and Songs. 1969. Methodist Publishing House, London.
New Church Praise. 1975. The Saint Andrew Press, Edinburgh, Scotland.
Pilgrim Praise. 1972. Fred Kaan. Galliard Ltd., Queen Anne's Road, Great Yarmouth,
    Norfolk, England.
Praise for Today. 1974. Psalms and Hymns Trust, 4 Southampton Row, London WC1B
    4AD.
Praise the Lord. 1972. Geoffrey Chapman, London.
Westminster Praise. 1976. Ed. by Erik Routley. Hinshaw Music, Inc., P. O. Box 470,
    Chapel Hill, N.C. 27514.
26 Hymns. 1971. F. Pratt Green. Epworth Press, 27 Marylebone Rd., London NW9 5JS.
100 Hymns for Today. 1969. William Clowes & Sons, Ltd., 14-16 Lower Regent Street,
    London, SW.
Worship II: A Hymnal for Roman Catholic Parishes. 1975. G.I.A. Publications, Inc., 7404
    South Mason Avenue, Chicago, IL 60638.

INDEX